8
Secrets of In
Success

Martin Hawes is one of New Zealand's most successful financial writers. A popular speaker at seminars and conferences he also serves on the boards of several companies.

After a brief period teaching, Martin set up an importing and manufacturing company which he ran for ten years. In 1986 he became a business and financial consultant. Editor of *Moneyline* since 1987 he contributes to several publications and is currently the money consultant for *North and South*.

Author of the definitive best-seller, *Family Trusts*, Martin's other books include *Save Money on Your Mortgage, Your Money Life-Line* and *Money and Divorce*.

He likes to climb mountains, run and ski.

I would like to acknowledge the work of Ralph Brown of Media Associates, Christchurch, and John Owen of Ord Minnett (sharebrokers) for their help and assistance with this book.

Martin welcomes comments and questions about all his books. Time constraints mean he may not always be able to reply. He can be contacted at: mhawes@gallarus.co.nz

SECRETS OF
INVESTMENT
SUCCESS

Martin Hawes

PENGUIN BOOKS
Penguin Books (NZ) Ltd, cnr Airborne and Rosedale Roads, Albany,
Auckland 1310, New Zealand
Penguin Books Ltd, 27 Wrights Lane, London W8 5TZ, England
Penguin USA, 375 Hudson Street, New York, NY 10014, United States
Penguin Books Australia Ltd, 487 Maroondah Highway, Ringwood, Australia 3134
Penguin Books Canada Ltd, 10 Alcorn Avenue, Toronto, Ontario,
Canada M4V 3B2

Penguin Books Ltd, Registered Offices: Harmondsworth, Middlesex, England

First published by Penguin Books (NZ) Ltd, 1998
3 5 7 9 10 8 6 4
Copyright © Martin Hawes, 1998

The right of Martin Hawes to be identified as the author of this work in terms of
section 96 of the Copyright Act 1994 is hereby asserted.

Typeset by Egan-Reid Ltd
Printed in Australia by Australian Print Group, Maryborough

CONTENTS

FOREWORD

I CANNOT RECALL A PERIOD DURING WHICH THE SUBJECT OF personal investment and financial planning has been so topical.

This is, perhaps, due to a fundamental change in most people's perceptions about retirement. The old belief that leaving the workforce must be accompanied by a reduced standard of living is no longer accepted. As a result, there has been corresponding growth in the number of investment options available and often conflicting advice about the benefits of a particular choice.

In explaining the eight basic 'secrets' of investment, Martin Hawes provides a balanced perspective of the positive and negative aspects of a range of options, including shares and real estate.

The clarity of his presentation is enhanced by the inclusion of a glossary of investment terms and an investment directory. These provide a valuable reference to many commonly used, and sometimes misunderstood, concepts.

While the ultimate investment decision rests with the individual, Martin's book provides an informed and critical appraisal of the available options and is a solid foundation for anyone intent on building wealth and financial independence.

Sir Ron Brierley

FIRST WORD

It's Your Money

INVESTMENT IS NOT ABOUT LUCK – IT IS NOT A GAME OF CHANCE. There are winners and losers in investment – people who make money and people who don't, and some who succeed at times and fail at others, never quite knowing why they are not consistent. Whatever the reason for poor performance, it has nothing to do with chance. Those who succeed with investments do not do so by accident.

The difference between performances is that those who succeed are those who know the secrets of investment and follow some basic rules – and keep on following them regardless of what happens. None of these rules is complicated; none of them particularly difficult; but they need to be known, understood and followed in a disciplined and consistent way.

Investment success for the average person does not require detailed knowledge and jargon, nor the right contacts and inside information, even though there is a public perception that that is what is needed. What is in fact required is a reasoned and rational approach, along with patience and discipline. The most successful investors are 'principled investors'. That does not mean that they favour 'green' or socially responsible investments – it means that they invest strictly according to the principles that they have set.

The most successful investors work hard and study detail. There is no quick, easy or lazy way to consistently good investment performance.

> **The most successful investors work hard and study detail.**

This may not sound very attractive – a sort of joyless, Calvinistic approach. Nevertheless, it is undoubtedly how people succeed. Most things that are worth having take some time and effort. In nearly everything you reap to the extent that you have sowed. Investment is no different – get-rich-quick schemes usually have the opposite result to what was promised.

The secrets contained in this book are not secrets in the sense that they are deliberately hidden or concealed – they are not. However, they are certainly secrets insofar as they are known by few (and used by even fewer) and you cannot hope to unravel the puzzle of investment without them. The secrets are the key to help the bewildered and bamboozled. Without them, the whole area of investment is an enigma in which you cannot hope to reasonably participate, let alone succeed.

To many people, investment (and finance generally) is like some incomprehensible religion complete with its own language, liturgy, gurus and priests. To these people it is so difficult and confusing that it is quite unapproachable. When they hear dark-suited prelates using terms like 'discounted cash flows', 'dealers' spreads', 'thick markets' and 'net present value' (all said very quickly), they feel that the whole thing is beyond them. To make matters worse, the priests themselves never seem to be able to agree as to what is the true path to investment heaven. Although I do not think that such experts necessarily use jargon deliberately to show how clever they are, it is nevertheless daunting for the uninitiated. Investment advisers and people like sharebrokers and fund managers have a lot to answer for in their inability and unwillingness to use language that those on the outside can follow.

There is no one successful path to investment heaven – no path that we can all be shown by some investment guru. I mistrust such ideas and their 'ways' to enlightenment, the personal followings that are built. Investment is an individual thing, each person with her own starting point, her own needs and her own aims. How she achieves these will be peculiar to her – one size does not fit all.

There is no one successful path to investment heaven.

There is also the question of trust – can you trust people's honesty and competency? Because the first thing that you must realise is this: if you are going to invest, you need to give your money to someone else. Whether you buy shares, buy property, put your money in the bank, invest in Government stock . . . you are going to have to give your (possibly) hard-earned money to another person. The only alternative is to put bank notes under the mattress.

There is no such thing as a risk-free investment.

There is no such thing as a risk-free investment. Even investing with the Government is not risk-free – governments have been known to have difficulties in the past and to renege on their obligations (although admittedly not often). There are degrees of risk in all investments – some have great risks, some small. If you give your money to someone else there is always a chance that you will not get it back.

How can you ever know who to trust? The answer is that you cannot completely trust anybody – you must have at least some control yourself, some knowledge of the principles of investment. Your money, how it is invested, how it is handled, cannot be a secret to you. Even if you are investing in managed funds, using the best financial advice available and paying someone to do your investing for you, you need to know at least the basics to understand what is going on. Investment does not need to be incomprehensible, a mystical craft revealed only to a few – and given its importance to you, nor should it be. I believe that people should know what they are getting into. After all, it's your money!

The difference between winners and losers is huge. The value of time is such that a relatively small difference in the return that you get from your investments will make a huge difference to your final position. Look at an example: two investors each invest $50,000. One gets an 8% return while the other gets 10%. After 20 years the first investor has $246,000 while the second investor has $366,000. The difference between an 8% return and a 10% return may not seem much – but the final result is! The investor with the additional $120,000 is going to enjoy life a lot more!

This example shows the difference with only a small disparity between the returns. We all know that returns can vary a good deal more than just 2%. Some investors that I know aim for 30% a year while others may invest in something which collapses and takes the investor's money with it down a big black hole. Perhaps nearly as bad is the situation common to so many people where they see their investments languish, apparently doing nothing, while the investor dimly recognises that something is wrong but does not know what to do about it. A 2% difference in return is quite small compared to what sometimes happens.

Even amongst professional investors, the fund managers who are highly trained and qualified and spend their entire working day trying to get the best returns for their investors, there is frequently great disparity in the results that they achieve. You can compare the returns that fund managers get their investors from New Zealand equities (shares) over a 3-year period and find that one might get 14% while another gets -3%.

With these sorts of differences, you need to know what is going on. You need to be able to pick investments which are if not the best, at least good.

The first thing that you must do, however, is get started – having decided to become a principled investor the sooner that you start the better off you will be. Starting may be a simple savings plan at your local bank or it may be the building of a share portfolio.

Whatever your choice, you need to make a conscious decision to get on with it, to learn about it and start making some investments.

The 8 secrets in this book with their principles properly followed will mean that you will be aware of the big picture, know what drives investment markets and be familiar with the particular markets that you are involved in. You should be able to see value in certain investments, even spot bargains, while discarding heavily promoted rubbish. Following a small number of rules, being a principled investor should at least stop you doing dumb stuff. Knowing these secrets will filter out the worst mistakes that you might make. The principles should see you maximise the returns from your investments. Even the use of a few of them should improve your returns and help to better the comfortable relationship between you and your money.

> **Being a principled investor should at least stop you doing dumb stuff.**

There are very profitable investments to be made with relatively low risk. Most successful investors are in fact not big risk-takers although on the surface they may appear to be (and the textbooks would consider them so). They may not, for example, have a diversified portfolio (something which does reduce risk), preferring instead to hold only a few top-performing investments. The reason that they can do this with safety is that they analyse their investments carefully, take a calm rational approach, and are patient and disciplined.

That is how successful investors work. Not everyone does have the same degree of knowledge nor the same skills. Some investments are better than others – there are genuine bargains (undervalued investments) out there, and there always will be. The best investors know how to identify them and take advantage of them. You can choose to be amongst them if that is what you want. At the very least, you can make investments that you are comfortable with, which fit in with your personality and circumstances and which will complement and enhance your lifestyle, rather than detract from it. Money may not be the source of all evil, but a lack of it can certainly be a cause of great unhappiness.

Your money is your responsibility, regardless of whether you are an experienced investor or just beginning. If you end up in rags while others have riches, or if your money fits unhappily with your lifestyle, you have no one to blame but yourself. You cannot blame the Government, the tax system, the vagaries of the sharemarket, your investment adviser, property valuer, sharebroker or even the crooked director of the company that you invested in. All of these are the same for all people and all investors. It was you who made the decision to give your money to someone else; you chose who to give it to.

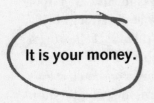

It is your money.

It is your money – and always your decision.

SECRET 1

There Are Only Three Investments

▼ ▼ ▼ ▼

'An investment must carry a return.'

THE WORD 'INVESTMENT' MUST BE ONE OF THE MOST abused in the English language. People talk about investing in gold, art, antiques, jewellery, investing in car registration plates and even investing at the TAB on a dog race. None of these is an investment.

An investment must carry a return. For something to be an investment there has to be an expected income from it. This income is generated by the investment asset; it is not from a change in value of the investment itself.

> **An investment must carry a return.**

Buying gold, art, antiques and car registration plates (or anything else for that matter) in the hope that it will go up in value is not investment – it is speculation. Putting money on a dog is gambling.

Defining these terms is not just a bit of academic interest (a study in semantics) – it is important to know precisely what it is that you are doing. You need to be able to get through all of the hype which surrounds the financial world. When someone asks you to 'invest' in a car number plate you need to know that you are not investing but speculating. The two words, 'invest' and 'speculate', have very different connotations and meanings. How many people would buy an 'Investment Plate' if they were called 'speculators' plates' (as they ought to be)?

Just as important to understand is that it is the cash return from investments which values investments – not the other way round. It is the sustainability and likely growth of the income which establishes the value that people will pay for investments in the marketplace.

When you boil things down, there are in fact only three things which give a cash return and therefore only three investments that you can make:

▼ **Interest-bearing deposits.** This is simply giving someone your money and getting interest from them for the use of your money.

▼ **Property.** Buying rental property (not bare land) for its income.

▼ **Business (or equities).** Buying all or part (by means of shares) of a business for its profits and dividends.

There are no investments other than these three – no other assets which carry a return and which give a sustainable cashflow.

These three investments can further be split into two categories: ownership and debt. Ownership is when you own the investment and take all of the profits; debt is when you lend to receive interest. Shares and property are ownership investments, interest-bearing deposits of all types are debt.

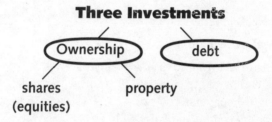

Over long periods of time, investment in ownership assets is likely to be more profitable – but it also has more risk. The potential return from ownership is open-ended. You may get a return which is (nearly) infinite – the sky is the limit. On the other hand, you may lose all of your money. The return from debt investments is fixed at the time that you make the investment. There is not going to be any great upside but nor is there likely to be much downside.

In any insolvency (liquidation, receivership or mortgagee sale), it is the owners who are paid out last. Those who have lent money for interest will be repaid their capital first. Even in non-insolvency situations, it is the people who have lent their money who get a return (their interest) first, regardless of whether or not there are any profits. The people with ownership get a return only if there are profits.

▼ SPECIAL NOTE: REAL RATE OF RETURN

The real rate of return is the return that you get after tax and inflation have been taken into account. In times of high tax and inflation it is very difficult to get a real rate of return – in the 1980s if you had your money in the bank you were actually getting poorer, such were the ravages of inflation and taxation at the time.

To calculate the real rate of return you simply take off the taxation first and then adjust for inflation.
For example:

Yield	7.5%
Less Taxation at 33%	(2.5%)
Return after Tax	5%
Less Inflation	(2%)
Real Rate of Return	**3%**

This investment is making the investor 3% richer each year. Certainly she is earning 5% after tax, but inflation is eroding her spending power by 2% each year. Therefore, after both taxation and inflation have been accounted for, her real rate of return is 3%.

So, what about other investments like unit trusts, super-annuation funds, group investment funds and managed funds generally? These are simply a **means** of investment, the vehicle through which you invest. Similarly with shares – whether listed on the sharemarket or not, shares are a method of investing in a business.

As soon as you realise that interest-bearing deposits, rental property and businesses are the only things that you can invest in, and that everything else is either speculation (which few people want any part of) or a means of investing (in the case of unit trusts and managed funds), many of the complications simply fall

Experience shows that calling the immediate direction of any market is a difficult gamble.

away. Fine art might be beautiful (and possibly go up in value), antiques might be rare (and possibly go up in value), car plates might be fun (and possibly go up in value) – but that does not make them investments. People buy investments for the income that they can get from them.

▼ SPECIAL NOTE: SPECULATION VS INVESTMENT

Investment is better than speculation because:

1. It is safer. Speculators are buying things which usually have little intrinsic value. They need to pick the direction of the market and the market needs to move that way promptly. Experience shows (and commonsense would tell you anyway) that calling the immediate direction of any market is a difficult gamble.
    Investors on the other hand have the income from their investments. If the market does not move their way immediately they have that cashflow to pay their borrowings or enjoy, as the case may be. Their investments have an intrinsic worth, established by the very cashflow that they are banking.

2. It is more profitable. This is so in two senses. The first is that the speculator will have a greater share of bad calls (and losses) to offset against his successful gambles. The principled investor will have far fewer of these, particularly as he can happily wait until the market moves in his direction, banking his income in the meantime. The second reason for increased profitability is that the cashflow from investments adds substantially to the overall return. The speculator who buys a section in the Coromandel or in Queenstown needs a lot more capital gain than the owner of a warehouse in East Tamaki or some flats in Merivale. The cash return, whether it is applied to pay for borrowings or simply spent, is a substantial and valuable part of any return.
    Clearly, clever investors try to pick the market correctly. However, they buy investments not items of little essential value and with no cashflow – and they can afford to wait.

Of course, each investment type has sub-categories.

PROPERTY

There are only four classes of property which represent pure property investments:

Residential	(flats)
Industrial	(warehouses)
Commercial	(offices)
Retail	(shops)

Only these four have income derived from tenants which is not related to one particular type of business. Hotels and motels are as much dependent on the success of the business as anything else, as are farms. As such they are not pure property plays. In part at least the success of owning any such property depends on how well the farming or accommodation industries perform.

Bare land is not, of course, an investment – it carries no cash return. Buying a section in the hope that it will rise in value is pure speculation.

Many houses fall into the same category. Their rent is so low compared to the purchase price that the 'investor' is dependent upon capital growth for her return. Recently I heard of an acquisition in Auckland which an 'investor' had purchased. The purchase price was $400,000 and the rent was $390 per week ($20,280 pa). After costs of rates, insurance and some maintenance the net rent was around $18,000 pa. This would give the 'investor' a cash return of 4.5% on his purchase price (before any capital gain). Without capital gain the 'investor' will do very poorly. The 'investor' is in fact entirely reliant on capital gain and is therefore not an investor at all, but a speculator.

> **Buying a section in the hope that it will rise in value is pure speculation.**

Although there are only four classes of property which represent a pure property investment, there are a number of ways and means to invest in property. As with the other two investment classes, there is a basic choice to be made between direct investment and managed investments – that is, whether you do the investing yourself or you pay someone to do it for you.

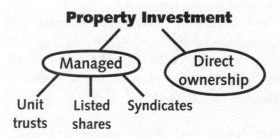

DIRECT PROPERTY INVESTMENT

Great numbers of New Zealanders have gone out and purchased rental properties directly themselves. By international standards, New Zealand has not only a very high proportion of people who own their own home but also a very large number of people who have purchased a property for rental. This high number of direct rental property investors is for a number of reasons: a Kiwi do-it-yourself attitude; the good performance of property as an investment over the last few decades; large numbers of books and seminars extolling the virtues of property investment; and the advantageous tax treatment of direct property investment.

All else being equal, you are better to invest directly yourself than go into property through managed funds. However, all else is seldom equal – there are many people who ought to have some exposure to property as an investment who cannot (or should not) own the property themselves.

MANAGED PROPERTY INVESTMENTS

There are two reasons why people buy into indirect property investments.

▼ **They lack the time or skill to invest themselves.** There are many direct property investors (especially those who invest in residential property) who would be horrified if they added up all of the time that they put into the purchase and management of their investments.

▼ **They lack the funds or capital to invest directly.** This is especially important for those who want exposure to commercial property – few people have the millions of dollars that are usually required to buy into office blocks in Auckland or Wellington.

There are three ways in which you can invest in property without having to put your name on a property title or manage it yourself.

Unit Trusts

Most fund managers (insurance companies, banks, trust companies, etc) have unit trusts based on property. Investors' funds are pooled and put into a trust which is then managed by the promoter. The manager purchases the properties and manages them for the trust to the best of its abilities (and of course charges a fee for doing so). The trust is then 'unitised' so that you can own units in the trust. The value of the units will rise (and fall) along with the value of the underlying property that the trust owns. Usually the income of the trust (from rentals) is paid out twice yearly to investors. Some property unit trusts are very large, owning hundreds of millions of dollars of property. Some of New Zealand's most well known, most prestigious and best properties are owned by unit trusts.

The great advantage of property unit trusts is their liquidity. Property unit trusts usually keep a good amount of cash in reserve enabling them to redeem the units of investors who want to cash up. However, you need to be aware that there is no guarantee of quick redemption of units. If large numbers of investors want out (as happened to the New Zealand Rural Property Trust and to several trusts in Australia), cash reserves might be insufficient, meaning that investors need to wait until the trust has sold some properties and has the cash to redeem units. This does not happen often – but it does happen. The liquidity of some property unit trusts is increased by the trust investing in property securities which are listed on the stock exchange. If the trust needs to cash up to some degree it is far easier to sell listed units than whole buildings.

The disadvantage of property unit trusts is the fees that are charged. The upfront fee could be as much as 5% with an ongoing fee charged by the manager of 2%. Usually the upfront fee can be negotiated down if you go direct to the fund manager (and sometimes even if you go through a broker). The 2% ongoing fee represents the costs of running the trust (and some profit for the fund manager). Many of these costs (things like bookkeeping and accounting, organising repairs and maintenance, etc) are borne by private investors anyway, although there is frequently little account taken of them.

Interestingly, all property unit trusts are based on commercial and industrial property. In spite of several attempts to launch them, there are none based on residential property. Ultimately the costs of purchasing and managing relatively low-value residential property are too great if calculated at full professional rates. Direct residential property investors should be aware of this – the huge amounts of time that they often put into their properties should have a value, if not in monetary terms then in terms of lifestyle.

> **Many of these costs are borne by private investors anyway, although there is frequently little account taken of them.**

Listed Property Shares

There are at least six companies or trusts listed on the New Zealand Stock Exchange whose main business and holdings are in property. This allows you to invest cheaply (1-2% brokers' fees) and easily into property. Better still, you can choose to invest into retail property (through St Lukes), commercial property (through AMP Office Trust), or industrial property (through Property For Industry). Again, there is no listed company based on residential property.

Most listed property shares pay quite good dividends, yielding perhaps 7-8% before tax. The companies often have small borrowings and pay most of their profits out in dividends. They usually trade a little below their asset backing; that is, there is no goodwill and often a discount on the underlying property values. This discount (or occasionally the premium) of the share price to the value of the underlying properties largely represents what the market believes to be the future prospects of the particular company's portfolio. The discount may also represent the disposal costs of the company's portfolio – that is, one day the company will need to sell its property and there will be costs (real estate agents' and legal fees) to sell them.

Investing in property through listed companies is advantageous to the extent that the investment is liquid – one call to your sharebroker with a sell order and you can cash up. However, you do need to be aware that listed property shares are subject to the vagaries of the sharemarket and can show some short-term volatility. While they will tend to track the value of the company's underlying property holdings over the long term, they may fluctuate over shorter periods.

Property Syndicates

There are many different forms of these, ranging from a few friends getting together and pooling their resources to buy property, through to quite large property syndicators like Waltus Investments Ltd who have very successfully purchased hundreds of millions of dollars of property with their clients. In between these extremes are financial planners, lawyers and accountants who have got their clients together to purchase property.

The real problem with syndicates is their lack of liquidity. Groups the size of Waltus can get around this by creating a secondary market where members sell their holdings if they need to. However, smaller groups are not usually so fortunate. Often

> **Be very wary of small property syndicates.**

syndicate investors will agree that they are in for the long term (perhaps 10 years). Nevertheless, people's circumstances change (marriage break-up, death of a spouse, illness, business difficulty, etc) requiring that investor to cash up. If he cannot find another syndicate member to buy his shares or perhaps find an outsider to do so, he is stuck with them. If the investor really wants to get rid of the shares he will probably have to substantially discount them. On the other hand, a situation can arise where over the years one member starts buying up other members' shares as they need to sell them. This member gradually becomes dominant as he holds the largest proportion of the syndicate even though the members started off with equal holdings. In time, that lone member may own half the shares and can dictate the direction of the syndicate.

I think you should be very wary of small property syndicates. Larger, specialist companies like Waltus have been very successful because they have been able to give some liquidity through a secondary market. They have also structured their syndicates well for tax purposes and have identified and purchased good properties which have performed well. Smaller, private syndicates often do not have these advantages – no secondary market and sometimes insufficient property investment and management skill.

▼ SPECIAL NOTE: PROPERTY SYNDICATE PITFALLS

Twelve people each put in $30,000 to buy a small commercial property. There was an unwritten agreement that the syndicate would stay together for at least 10 years. However, over the years some of the members needed to sell out – one bought a business, another's marriage broke up. The shares of these members were bought up by another member, usually at a discount. Over a period of about four years, this one member bought up about 40% of the shares in the syndicate. Then he wanted to build a new house – he needed to cash up too. Along with a couple of other members he voted to wind up the syndicate early. The property was sold (at about what it was purchased for), all the members got their money back, but with no great profit – except for the 40% holder. He made a profit because he had bought many of his shares at a discount.

While no great damage was done nor members disadvantaged, there were some who felt that a lot of trouble had been gone to for little reward. The syndicate had started on a jolly note but ended on a flat one.

SHARES

Buying shares is simply buying a part (or a share) of a business and its profits. Like property you can choose whether to do this directly yourself (on the sharemarket) or buy into a managed fund and have a manager do the investing for you.

Whichever way you choose to gain an exposure to equities, it is important that you think outside of New Zealand. New Zealand makes up only a tiny proportion (less than 1%) of the world's equity markets. By restricting yourself to New Zealand you are denying yourself access to some of the world's best companies in the world's best economies. Even Australia is not very big by world standards although it does give access to banking and resource stocks which are not available in New Zealand. The close economic relationship between New Zealand and Australia means that simply investing there provides little diversification.

It is that diversification which makes offshore investment so important. Investing only in New Zealand is like living in Paeroa and investing only in Paeroa properties and businesses. This would be to ignore all of the other industries, properties and

Investing only in New Zealand is like living in Paeroa and Investing only in Paeroa.

companies that are in New Zealand but not in Paeroa. That is not sensible – nor is it sensible to limit investment to New Zealand, to the exclusion of the rest of the world.

Whether investing in New Zealand or internationally the first choice to make is whether to invest directly yourself or through a managed fund.

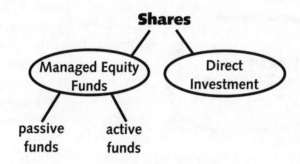

DIRECT SHARE INVESTMENT

This requires financial, business and investment skill (or very good and trustworthy advice). It also requires (more importantly) considerable discipline. There are many people who find the sharemarket frighteningly fickle. To them it is a sort of rich man's casino complete with its own incomprehensible jargon and where only those in the know are allowed to play.

I do not believe that the sharemarket is a gambling den at all. Like gambling there are risks but unlike gambling these risks can be substantially reduced with knowledge. Nor do I think that this knowledge is beyond most people – it is not. Provided that you keep in mind many of the fundamental principles that are outlined in this book (particularly the quest for sustainable and growing income), sharemarket jargon and behaviour are quite accessible. More problematic for many people is the disciplined and rational approach that is required (and which is a major theme of this book).

Most important of all for sharemarket investors is that they keep firmly in mind that they are buying into a business. Buying shares is not like buying commodities (tin, silver, coffee, etc). Understand that business as if it were the only thing that you owned. Who are your competition? What is happening in the marketplace? Do you have the right plant and equipment? These are the things that dictate buy or sell decisions in the sharemarket, not lines on a graph, the blind acceptance of a broker's recommendation or a tip at the club. Buying shares is buying a business.

Getting started in direct sharemarket investment is like getting started on any daunting project. You should prepare as far as you can by reading and listening to everything available. However, ultimately you have to get in and try – making mistakes perhaps, but learning from them. Shares allow you the luxury of doing this very slowly at the start. You can (and should) invest just a little at the beginning, increasing your investment gradually as time goes on and experience, knowledge, skill and judgement increase. There is a lot to learn – much of it you will only learn properly through experience, by being in the market.

> **Buying shares is buying a business.**

MANAGED FUNDS

Many people will never have the skills, the discipline, the time or the interest to invest themselves in the sharemarket. Fortunately there are fund managers who have these things and who you can pay to do it for you. This is especially important with international equities. While it is perhaps easy enough for most people to invest directly in New Zealand or even Australia, it is considerably harder to do so in other countries. Information is not as readily available and much of the procedure and jargon is different (for example, only in New Zealand and Australia are equities called 'shares' – in other countries they are called 'stocks'). Most people going into international equities will use one of the many unit trusts which are designed for that purpose.

Sharemarket managed funds work in the same way as property funds. Investors pay into the fund, the fund manager selects and purchases shares and charges a fee, and the investors enjoy the profits (or rue the losses as the case may be – in fact you should probably expect losses approximately one year in every six).

However, there are two distinct types of sharemarket managed funds: active funds and passive funds. There has been a debate going on between the proponents and promoters of each as to which is better. My view is that passive funds are better for the bulk of most people's sharemarket investment.

Active Funds

Active funds are the older type of sharemarket fund where the fund manager actively identifies and selects shares which it believes will do well. A good active fund manager will have a strong research section and its analysts will go out to companies and interview management and analyse prospects in detail. An active fund manager is active in buying and selling shares.

However, this has two consequences. The first is that these fund managers pay tax on their capital gains. The second is that the analysis and research are costly, making the fees charged by the manager necessarily higher.

> **The advent of passive funds will make active fund managers work even harder.**

Active fund managers work hard to get their investors the best return possible. Some manage to beat the relevant sharemarket index (say, the NZSE 40 capital index) but in fact many do not beat the index after tax and fees are taken out. This inability of most active fund managers to even get an average index return for its investors led to the development of passive funds. I think that the advent of passive funds will make active fund managers work even harder to the benefit of investors.

▼ SPECIAL NOTE: ADVISING THE ADVISERS

There are literally hundreds, probably thousands of managed investments in New Zealand. Some are good, some are average, some are, well . . .

How can you ever know which ones to choose?

This is a problem not only for the average investor but also for investment advisers and financial planners. They may be advising their clients to invest in offshore equities but there are scores of funds available. Which ones are likely to perform?

A few financial planners do their own research (and the two that I know in New Zealand do it very well). However, the vast majority of financial planners and advisers purchase research from either FPG Research or IPAC Securities. These two competing firms are full-time researchers, continually scrutinising and analysing managed funds and investments. They then sell their research to the firms of financial advisers and planners. Before ever acting on advice from a financial planner, check whether they do their own research (and if they do, do they do it well?) or buy research in from IPAC or FPG. Without good research, fund selection is no more than a shot in the dark.

Passive Funds

Passive fund managers do not even try to beat the index – all they do is track (or match) the index that the fund is based on. Because these managers are passive, their costs and fees are low. Better still, because they are not buying shares with the intention and purpose of selling them at a profit (ie, trading), they pay no tax on their capital gains. This gives them a considerable advantage.

An index is a portfolio of shares in proportion to the sizes of the companies that comprise it. A passive index fund buys the shares in the index in the proportion that they are in the index, and only buys and sells subsequently as the companies which make up the index change. This is all done by computer. There are a lot of different indices and passive index funds have sprung up to track many of them. Most have been received with great favour by investors and large amounts of money have gone into them.

However, in spite of the popularity of passive funds, there are some people who refuse to accept that they are better. The arguments go:

▼ A passive fund will only ever give an average market return. There is no scope for the fund manager to add value.

My answer to that is to look at the past performance of the active sharemarket fund managers – on average, after tax and fees, they seldom do much better than the market average. In fact, given that they have such high costs and tax to pay, they do very well to come anywhere near the market average. An average return from a passive fund is better than a below-benchmark return from an active fund!

▼ While passive funds might perform better in a rising market, they can take no defensive position in a falling market. Passive index-tracking funds must simply follow the market down. Active funds on the other hand can sell shares and hold cash in a bear market or use synthetics and futures contracts to hedge their position.

My answer to that is threefold:

• *The passive fund will have to go down with the market but because there have always been more rises than falls in equity markets, over long periods of time the investor will be better off.*

• *The active fund manager needs to be able to recognise that it is in a bear market and the extent and length of the downside. Assuming the fund manager has been able to recognise that it is in a down market (and some of them do not have great track records in that regard) it then has to be able to sell down. Some fund managers hold large parcels of certain shares – so large that they may not be able to quickly sell out at a reasonable price.*

• *Although the tracking fund itself may not be able to sell out of its holdings you, the investor, can sell out of the fund!*

I believe that people looking for managed sharemarket investments should have a large part of their money in passive funds. The balance could be in one or two carefully selected active funds or held directly in companies of the investor's liking. I would go further and say that even investors who are happy to invest directly themselves may be advantaged by having a substantial part of their investment in an index fund. Many direct sharemarket investors have perhaps half of their money in six or eight market leaders, good solid heavy-weights which make up a large proportion of most indices anyway and accordingly perform roughly the same as the index. The other half of such people's funds are in smaller companies or special situations where the investor can see value and profit. Given that the index funds are relatively cheap and are tax-efficient, it makes sense for people to save themselves time and administration hassles by having 50% of their funds in an index tracker (instead of in six or eight heavyweights) and the balance still in those special situations.

> I personally have some of my sharemarket funds in a passive index-tracker.

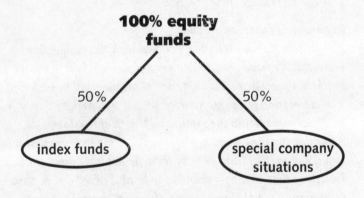

I think that this is a very reasonable way to invest in equities. Although I have all the skill necessary to invest directly into the sharemarket, as a time-saver I personally have some of my sharemarket funds in a passive index-tracker.

EXAMPLE:

Karen had received an inheritance of $50,000. She already owned her own house and another rental property. She had a good income from her job. She wanted to invest in equities partly to balance her property holdings and partly because she found the idea of shares quite exciting.

Karen's job and other activities kept her busy, meaning that a portfolio of 10–12 shares (including the leaders) was not really appropriate. After discussions, the following investments were made:

$25,000	Passive index fund	} Good exposure to market overall and to leaders
$10,000	International equities (2 trusts-$5000 each)	} Easiest and best way to get offshore equities
$5000	Telstra	
$5000	GPG	} Three companies which are long-term holdings and could outperform the market
$5000	Restaurant Brands	

The key to this portfolio is the use of the passive index fund which gives good cheap exposure without having the administration and market-watching requirements of six or eight leading shares.

INTEREST-EARNING DEPOSITS

Most people think of these as simply putting their money in the bank. That is a reasonable course – but interest-earning deposits are far more than that.

There are two main forms of debt investments:

Short Term Deposits

These are things like bank and finance companies deposits, where generally investments are for less than a year to two. There are also other debt investments such as deposits in lawyers' nominee mortgage companies (which are becoming rarer), family loans and bank bills. Bank bills are for larger sums of money (over $100,000), are for a set term (30, 60, 90 or 180 days) and are traded actively and continuously on the market. When you invest you will get the going interest rate at that particular time, which could change the minute after you make the investment (either up or down). You get a piece of paper which is like a post-dated cheque, redeemable on a certain day with the interest added on. So if you invested $250,000 for 60 days on 17 May you would get a cheque for say $253,333, dated 16 July. On 16 July you can redeem it at that higher value or roll it over for another period if you want.

Bonds

These are fixed-interest investments usually for longer periods of time, perhaps three years plus. In New Zealand bonds are often called 'stock' as in Government Stock or debenture stock. Bonds are issued by companies and corporations, local body authorities and governments. They pay a fixed rate of interest and as such are useful for people who need certainty of income. They are usually (although by no means always) low risk and have a secondary market where they can be sold by investors who need to cash up.

Although many people invest in interest-earning deposits themselves directly (there is little skill required), there is an increasing number of people getting higher returns by investing in debt markets through managed funds. There are three main types of these:

Fixed Interest or Bond Trusts

These are unit trusts which invest in fixed-interest securities both in New Zealand and internationally. The fund managers may trade bonds, timing the sale and purchase to best advantage for the fund. These funds usually give fairly good returns although they can make capital losses if interest rates rise. They are especially good for those who want access to offshore bond markets.

Mortgage Income Trusts

These trusts invest in mortgages: residential, commercial and farm. They will often give a higher return than bank deposits, after the manager's costs.

Cash Management Trusts

These invest in bank bills and similar securities, operating on the wholesale markets where individuals with relatively small amounts of money cannot invest. The investors' funds in these trusts are effectively on call and can usually be accessed by telephone transfer. They often give slightly higher returns than bank deposits.

All of these alternatives to the more usual bank deposits or bond purchasing are worth considering. However, it needs to be recognised that the risk in some of them may be slightly higher than bank deposits and there could also be some inconvenience in setting them up and accessing them. Of course there is also some cost involved for payment of the managers and trustee of the fund.

While there are only three investments, there are some hybrids of them which need to be mentioned. The first of these are *preference shares*. They are a combination of a fixed-interest investment (because they pay a fixed rate of interest for their term) and an equity investment (because the investor can often convert her securities to shares at the end of the term if she wishes). The holder of preference shares gets paid interest in preference to the ordinary shareholders getting a dividend and in the event of the company going into liquidation receives her capital back in preference to the ordinary shareholders. There are several different types of preference shares, some giving the holder the option to either receive their investment back in cash at the end of the term or convert it to ordinary shares in the company.

The other hybrid is the *balanced* or *diversified managed fund*. Such funds hold a range of investments designed to spread risk for the long-term investor. The asset allocation of a typical diversified fund might be:

Cash	10%
Property	20%
NZ equities	15%
International equities	15%
Mortgages	10%
NZ bonds	20%
International bonds	10%
	100%

The proportions may change a little over time or according to whether the fund manager is looking for growth or income and what degree of risk is acceptable. Nevertheless, note that these diversified funds are still based on investments – there is no holding of gold, antiques, art or car registration plates.

SECRET 2

Suit Yourself

▼ ▼ ▼ ▼

*'Match your own personality and
circumstances to the range of
investments that are available.'*

QUITE OFTEN A RELATIVE STRANGER WILL ASK ME: 'I've got a spare $10,000 – what should I do with it?' The questioner is really asking for a tip, something which will make him a big profit, preferably overnight. However, it is an unreasonable question because although I might know a share investment that represents good value and is likely to do well, or a well-structured property syndicate, I do not know the enquirer's circumstances, personality or financial situation. Investment is much more than just looking for a quick profit.

> **Investment is much more than just looking for a quick profit.**

There is a process which all principled investors must undertake. That process is the matching of your own personality and circumstances to the range of investments that are available. This may seem obvious but it is something which many people get wrong. It is a secret which is so essential that no one can be a successful long-term investor without it.

There is a debate which frequently rages as to which is the best investment – shares or property, bank deposits or bonds. This is a stupid argument and one that I refuse to buy into. The protagonists

> **All investment types have their place and purpose.**

in this debate are so keen to sell their own particular line that they miss a major principle of investment – that different investments suit different people in different situations. All investment types have their place and purpose. In my experience, those pushing one type of investment to the exclusion of others usually have a vested interest – they are selling something. In their drive for sales, common sense and logic are the first casualties.

Good investment is not simply hunting out the best returns available. If that were true it would make the science of investment much easier. It would be easier because we could all invest in the same thing. If all of our needs were the same, there would not be the plethora of investments available – one investment would suit everyone. A consensus of opinion would accept that a certain asset or investment product provided the best return and we would all put our money into that.

Clearly (some might say, regrettably) that is not the case. There are a lot of investments available and the reason is that each has been developed to suit particular circumstances. The way for you to take advantage of the fact that there are so many investment possibilities is to be sure that the investments that you make match and fit your particular situation. To do this you need to consider yourself, your personality and circumstances, and to weigh these against the range of investments available. Only by knowing these two things (yourself and the investments available) can you hope to make a good fit.

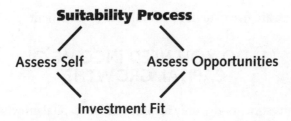

Suitability Process

Assess Self   **Assess Opportunities**

Investment Fit

The suitability process needs to be undertaken very carefully and accurately to get a good and happy fit. You must look honestly both at yourself and the investments that are available.

YOU – AS AN INVESTOR

You must make an assessment of yourself across a range of issues. Some of these relate to your circumstances and situation (and are therefore relatively easy), while others relate to your personality and character (which may be more difficult for some to confront).

The assessment needs to be done as honestly and as objectively as possible. Because of the objectivity required you may not be able to do this successfully yourself. Financial planners should be skilled in this area but if you have no wish to approach a professional,

> **If you fudge or gloss over hard issues, the only person being fooled is yourself.**

work some of the issues through with your partner, a friend or a relative who knows you well and will not be afraid to contradict what you might think or say.

There are two major things which are crucial in this self-assessment:

▼ **Honesty.** If you fudge or gloss over hard issues, the only person being fooled is yourself. As the fool, you are the only person being disadvantaged.

▼ **Sooner, rather than later.** By preference you should do this before you ever invest a dollar. It may seem boring and time-wasting as you are impatient to get started and chase high returns – but I think it is too important to skip over lightly.

There are five main factors in this self-assessment.

① DO YOU NEED INCOME OR CAPITAL GROWTH?

Some investments give only income (and no capital growth) while others give largely capital growth and little income. These usually work inversely, ie, the higher the likely income, the less the capital growth (and vice versa).

You should assess your need for income or capital growth on the basis of your tax position and your cash requirements for daily living. This is an important decision. For example, if you are a 40-year-old earning a very good income from your job (and on the top marginal tax rate) you probably do not want more income which would be heavily taxed. In this case you could consider going into a forestry partnership or perhaps direct property investment where the borrowings are so high that the property produces a tax loss (called negative gearing, see page 150). Someone in retirement, however, may want some income so would invest in bonds or perhaps ungeared property or high-dividend shares.

The advantage of high-dividend shares and ungeared property is that the income from them will probably show some growth. Investments like property and shares grow in two ways: they show capital growth (a rise in value of the investments themselves) but the income grows as well. Obviously the two are related. People in retirement, with no income other than that from their investments, may be in that situation for as long as 30 years or more. They cannot, therefore, ignore inflation and own only investments which give income. They need at least some capital – and income-growth investments as well.

Income or Growth?

Income	Growth
• deposits and bonds	• geared property
• high-dividend shares	• shares
• ungeared property partnership	• forestry

▼ SPECIAL NOTE: CAPITAL GAINS TAX

New Zealand is alone in the OECD in that it has no capital taxes. Most developed countries have a capital gains tax, including Australia which introduced one in 1985. The Australian capital gains tax is comprehensive – the only exemptions are the family residence and a few other relatively minor personal effects. Tax is paid on the capital profit on sale of an investment at the taxpayer's usual rate of tax. There is however an adjustment made for inflation – only the growth in the investment above the rate of inflation is taxed.

Although New Zealand does not have a capital gains tax (yet!) that does not mean that the sale of investments is always exempt from tax. There are two circumstances where the sale of investments can give rise to a tax liability.

The first of these is the sale of a bond (like Government stock) at a profit (see page 75, 76). Although the bond is sold to another investor on an arm's-length basis, the profit on the sale is deemed to be income and is therefore taxable.

The second circumstance concerns people who are traders, rather than investors. This is an important distinction that all investors should know about if they are not to receive an unexpected (and unpleasant) note from the IRD. The profits of traders are taxable (and any losses deductible), regardless of what asset they trade. The profits of investors are not taxable.

> **Your intention at the time of purchase is all-important.**

The difference between a trader and an investor is the person's intention at the time of making the purchase. If someone buys an asset with the intention of selling it on at a profit, she is a trader and should pay tax on her profits. However, if someone buys the same asset with the intention of holding it long term for its income (and for the growth in that income), then any capital profit on sale of the asset is deemed to be an unexpected (albeit fortunate) side benefit and is not therefore taxable.

Someone who buys something with the intention of selling it on is deemed to be in the business of buying and selling (like a retailer) and is therefore taxed on the profits. For example, you might buy a car for your own private use. You run around in the car for a while but after a few weeks decide to sell it. If you were lucky enough to sell the car at a profit, that profit would not be taxable. Your neighbour on the other hand might have bought a car cheaply with the intention of on-selling it at a profit. Even though he also uses the car privately for a while, because of his intention at the time of purchase, he would be deemed to be in the business of buying and selling cars and like a car dealer would be taxed on the profits.

Buying and selling investment assets (shares and property) is just the same. A trader is in the business of buying and selling shares and/or property – an investor is in the business of obtaining rental or dividend income.

Your intention at the time of purchase is all-important

– it dictates which category you are in. Of course intention can be difficult to prove either way – especially with the passage of time. After all, intention is a state of mind. Actions are usually (although not always) the best indicator of someone's intentions. Therefore a continual track record of buying properties or shares and selling them soon after purchase and at a profit would be the IRD's first indicator that you were a trader rather than an investor.

> **I have always thought that stagging shares is a very profitable sideline for investors.**

However, such a track record is by no means the end of the question. It is not that you buy and sell shortly after purchase that is at issue – anything could have intervened to motivate you to sell sooner than you had thought. The only truly important matter is why you bought the investments and what was in your mind at the time.

One group who will be assessed for tax on the sale of their shares are those who 'stag' new issues. In sharemarket terms, a stag is one who takes up shares in a new company float planning to sell them as soon as the company lists on the sharemarket. For example, in late 1997 Sky TV sold off some of its shares to the public at 240¢ and listed on the sharemarket both in New Zealand and the USA. On listing the shares traded at 270¢ – a 30¢ profit for the stags (those who sold them immediately). However, that profit would have been reduced because it would be taxed.

I have always thought that stagging shares is a very profitable sideline for investors. In fact I believe that investors should try to buy some of every new share that is going to list. (The exception is shares in property companies which often list at or even a little lower than the issue price.) Although not all shares will give a profit to the stags, experience shows that the majority do – the occasional failure will be more than made up for by the successes. However, stags must be prepared to pay tax on their stagging profits – by definition, stags are buying with the intention of selling on.

② HOW LONG WILL YOU WAIT FOR A RETURN?

Some investments give a return in one day (eg, bank deposits) while others might take 25 years to reach their full potential (eg, forestry, property and some superannuation policies). You need to be very clear about the length of time for which you are investing.

Forced sales are almost always unprofitable. You always want to be in a position so that you can choose the time of cashing up an investment. Of course, it may be that your circumstances change (divorce, death of a spouse, illness, etc) causing you to need to cash up. However, within normal circumstances you should know for how long you are making each investment.

Getting this wrong has caused many people financial grief. I have seen people put short-term money (actually their tax money) into the sharemarket. I have witnessed others lose substantial amounts of money and time on superannuation policies (see Special Note). Some unit trusts charge a fairly high upfront fee (eg, property and equity trusts) and you need to be in these for a sufficient length of time so that the fee is well spread over the years.

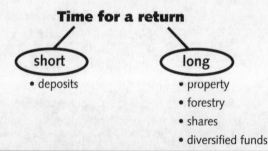

Time for a return

short
- deposits

long
- property
- forestry
- shares
- diversified funds

▼ SPECIAL NOTE: SUPER POLICIES

The importance of getting the right fit can be seen over and over again in people's personal experiences. It is not just investing for the wrong time period (and having to sell early at a loss), nor buying the wrong investment and paying too much tax. Worse by far is spending years going down the wrong investment path and losing both time and opportunity.

This happens with different investment types, but nowhere does it happen more often than with certain types of superannuation policies – those which have very high upfront fees. This sort of policy was very common some years ago. Although they are less popular now they are still heavily promoted and sold by some companies.

Such policies are usually for long periods of time, typically 20-30 years. The investor puts in an amount each month and at the end of the period receives a very large benefit. While the money is going in, the superannuation company invests the funds, usually in a good solid diversified portfolio.

Like any managed fund, the manager (the superannuation company in this case) needs to be paid for managing your money. With this kind of policy most of the management fee is taken at the start of the investment. Often all of the premiums that you pay in for the first year (or even longer) are taken for fees (a large part of which goes to pay the salesman who sold the policy to you). After that fee has been deducted, the annual fees charged are actually quite small. In fact provided you keep the policy going for the prescribed time (maybe 25 years) the total fees charged might be very reasonable.

> **It is when you do not keep it going that such a policy turns out to be a lousy deal.**

It is when you do not keep it going (you decide to cash up before maturity for some reason) that such a policy turns out to be a lousy deal. In effect you have paid for 25 years of management in advance, but because you are getting out early you do not receive the management for which you have prepaid.

This is the reason why some people in cashing up after a few years find that they do not even get their money back, let alone any interest or return. Someone who has paid in say $15,000 over seven years might only get back $13,000. Worse than that, they have lost years of growing their wealth and missed opportunities. Sometimes investors get angry with the insurance company about this – but their anger should usually be directed at themselves, not the company (or salesman) who sold them the policy.

They should be angry because they broke a cardinal rule of investment – they did not suit themselves. They did not buy into an investment which would fit their circumstances for its entire duration. In my view these policies are so inflexible that there are few people today for whom they would have any use. Lifestyles often change several times over the course of a working life – to effectively lock yourself into a 25-year investment (and prepay the costs of that investment) lacks the flexibility to suit many people. The superannuation companies will of course tell you that this kind of policy provides discipline but it is a discipline that is applied from outside and therefore not nearly as good or as lasting as self-discipline. Most investors need flexibility far more than they need an imposed regime. Fortunately there are many superannuation companies, banks and fund managers who offer far more flexible super policies and investments where you pay the fees as you go rather than upfront as a lump sum.

③ HOW MUCH RISK CAN YOU TOLERATE?

You need to know the degree of risk that you can handle, emotionally as well as financially. Your financial position is important in that if you have a good solid financial base you can afford to have a few high-risk/high-return investments. If you do not have a strong financial base, you need to resist the temptation to speed things up by taking risks, hard though that may be. Age may also make a difference – someone aged 60 will almost certainly want less risky investments than someone who is 35. The aggressive 35-year-old has more time to recover financially from a major mistake and is therefore likely to be more prepared to take some risk.

However, your financial position is not the only factor. If you tend to worry about money (and do not sleep well at night) you should stay away from risky investments (speculative gold-mining shares are not sleep-promoting). On the other hand, there are people who enjoy some excitement which they are unlikely to get from a 25-year superannuation policy. This person enjoys watching the value of his shares move around and is stimulated by the cut-and-thrust of the market. For someone like that an investment in a 25-year superannuation policy will simply end up getting boring and will be cashed up early (and at a loss).

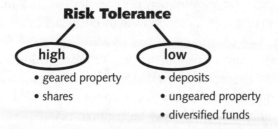

People who are worried by risk will have their judgement clouded.

The emotional side of risk assessment can be important for two reasons. The first is that money and investment are there to serve you and to make you happy. This does not happen if you have the wrong fit and are worried about your investments. The second is that you do not want your emotions (fear, greed or even boredom) to get in the way of your investment decisions. People who are worried by risk will have their judgement clouded. Investment decisions need to be made with the head – and a clear one at that! Emotion should not come into it.

Risk Tolerance

high	low
• geared property	• deposits
• shares	• ungeared property
	• diversified funds

▼SPECIAL NOTE: KEEP LIQUID

Everyone should have their affairs arranged so that they always have the ability to write a good-sized cheque. We should all have some liquid assets or an undrawn credit facility as a fighting fund against adverse events.

As a general rule this should be no less than 10% of your total annual income – ie, at least a month's income.

This income includes rents and dividends as well as salary. Property investors (especially those who are negatively geared) should have considerably more liquidity than just one month's income – three months or even six months may be more appropriate for some people.

Not all people will have this liquidity on deposit in a bank or cash management trust. Those who have borrowings will instead be better off by having an undrawn revolving credit facility. This is like an overdraft and will allow you to draw funds in times of low cashflow or emergency.

④ WHAT LEVEL OF INVESTMENT SKILL DO YOU HAVE?

Investment does require some skill. Much of this skill will in fact flow from your level of interest in financial and investment matters. There is little in investment and finance that most people cannot learn – if they are interested. One thing which puts some people off learning about investment is the idea that it necessarily involves difficult mathematics. In fact it does not – it generally only involves arithmetic: adding, subtracting, dividing and multiplying. While some professional investors may use complex statistical modelling for fund management, most private investors need only the four basic functions of arithmetic.

However, some investments require more arithmetical skill than others. The formulae to value bonds on the secondary market is more complicated than the arithmetic of property investment.

The other skill which may be required is interpersonal and communication competence. Clearly no communication or interpersonal skill is required in some investments – shares only require that you are able to say 'Buy Carter Holt Harvey' and interest-bearing deposits require form-filling rather than personal communication or negotiation. However, one area that does require good interpersonal skills is property investment. The best and most successful property investors are good negotiators. They negotiate the purchase of their properties, they negotiate with their bank and with their tenants and they negotiate the sale of their properties. These are people who are very good at getting their own way, sometimes manipulating others to do so.

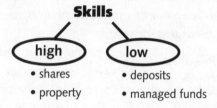

5) HOW MUCH TIME ARE YOU PREPARED TO DEVOTE TO YOUR INVESTMENTS?

The amount of time that you are prepared to devote to your investments is a critical part of your self-assessment. Property and shares are usually quite time-demanding. Property requires time not just to identify, negotiate, finance and purchase but to manage as well. Having said that, you can, if you wish, pay someone to manage your investment property. This will cost around 7-8% of rentals for residential property and considerably less for other types of property. I do not believe that management of your property should necessarily put you off owning investment property directly.

Shares will also require your time. This time will be spent not just on identifying, analysing and then purchasing good shares but also in administering and watching over them. Even those investors who buy shares and put them in the bottom drawer 'forever' must still be aware of what is happening within the market in general and in their companies in particular. This along with banking dividend cheques, reading accounts, filing reports, etc, does take time.

Most interest-bearing deposits require little attention although some investors do spend considerable time and energy shopping around for the best interest rates. An increasing number of investors are finding that the best interest rates with little additional risk come not from banks but from the cash management unit trusts which are offered by some fund managers. These can return a full 1% over the rates that banks offer – a gap that over the years will represent a great deal of money for you.

Decide on the amount of time that you are prepared to devote to your investments and then choose the most appropriate area. If, for example, you are a very busy person with two jobs, three children, are on the local council and like to run marathons, you should probably keep away from property investment (or at least have someone manage it for you).

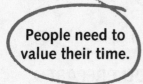

People need to value their time.

Many people need to value their time. If you put a proper monetary value on the time spent looking after your investments, you may find that you are in fact better off to pay someone to look after them for you (ie, invest through managed funds). For example, if you are paid $40 per hour and can earn that whenever you want, you may be better off carrying on working and investing through a unit trust. This is paying someone else to do what she is good at (funds management) while you work (and earn accordingly) at what you are good at. It may be that this does not suit you – for many people their investments are an interest and a welcome break from work. In addition, some people like the feeling of control that they have when they do not need to rely on others. However, the decision as to whether or not to invest directly yourself or have a fund manager do it for you is not solely related to your investment ability and skill.

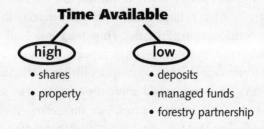

Time Available

high
• shares
• property

low
• deposits
• managed funds
• forestry partnership

▼ SPECIAL NOTE: RECORD-KEEPING

There are many for whom the detailed minutiae of keeping books and records, managing and administering, is a pain. There are people, usually with an entrepreneurial bent, who may be able to research and analyse in detail quite happily but who fail consistently to keep their files and records in order. They are often too busy doing 'important' things and finding their next great investment to be bothered tidying up after the purchase of their last one.

People need to recognise their skills or weaknesses in this area. The keeping of good files and records is important. It is important for tax purposes, it is important for performance measurement and important for research and analysis. It makes no sense to recognise great investments but to have your affairs in a shambles.

If you fall into this category there are a number of things that you can do about it. You can have fewer investments. You can consider using some sort of managed fund for the majority of your equity exposure rather than owning 12 different shares, or to go into managed funds through a Master Trust (see page 189). You can of course have any property holdings managed for you and if necessary have someone (partner or possibly employee) do the filing and record-keeping for you.

Administration is important even if you do find it boring. Recognise any weakness that you may have in this area and do something about it. Organisation is ultimately far more efficient and pleasant than a shambles.

TYPES OF INVESTMENTS

The three investment types each have different attributes and give different benefits to an investor. To properly go through the matching process you need to not only know yourself but also to know which investment will best suit your situation, and why.

The following chart outlines the attributes, advantages and disadvantages of different investments.

INVESTMENT COMPARISON			
	Deposits	Equities/Shares	Property
Risk	low	high	med
Tax Efficiency	low	med	high
Cash Income	high	med	med
Capital Growth	low	high	high
Return Period	1 day +	12 months +	5 years +
Time Involved	low	med	high
Arithmetical Skills	med	high	med
Interpersonal Skills	low	low	high

Note this chart represents averages only. The different investments will have these attributes and perform as in the chart in the majority of circumstances – but there are plenty of exceptions.

PROPERTY

The chart shows property investment characteristics in most situations and relates to the way that most people go about it. However, you can alter things by gearing up highly (borrowing a large proportion of the purchase price) to buy property, or on the other hand borrowing very little.

If you have a lot of borrowings, your tax efficiency will be high but your cash income will be lower. At the same time, your risk will be changing from medium to high. If you borrow very little your tax efficiency will be much lower, as will be your capital growth and your risk, but your income will be much higher.

In addition the attributes of property can depend on what you buy and where you buy it. For example, residential property tends to be less volatile than commercial property. Residential property also requires more of your time to manage than industrial property and tends to give lower income than other types.

> **Properties in poor locations are usually sold on very high yields.**

Some properties give higher income and lower capital growth, and vice versa. This is usually dictated by their location. There is normally a trade-off between income and growth in all investment types – few investments give good growth and good yield when they are purchased. Property investment is no exception – properties in poor locations are usually sold on very high yields. In fact the vendor has to pitch the price low to give a high yield if he is going to quit the property. A property in a small low-growth town out in the provinces is likely to show little capital growth (in fact there is a good chance that it might decline in value, as is happening in many rural and provincial centres in New Zealand). It will therefore have to be offered on a very high yield (perhaps 15-20%) simply to find a buyer. A property in a major centre (Auckland, Christchurch, Hamilton, etc) will generally sell on a lower yield because there are good prospects for both rental and capital growth there.

This trade-off may mean that the total projected returns from a small-town property may be roughly the same as those from a big city. A property in Cricklewood might be purchased on a 15% yield (with no capital growth) while one in Tauranga might be purchased on a 10% yield (but with 5% probable capital growth).

	Cricklewood	Tauranga
Income Yield	15%	10%
Capital Growth	_nil_	_5%_
	15%	15%

In fact, if our property markets were properly efficient, you would expect projected returns to be the same in all centres – all information would be factored in to property prices. However, two things

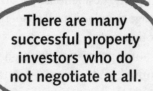

There are many successful property investors who do not negotiate at all.

need to be kept in mind before we could say that it ought not to matter where we buy our properties. The first is there is far greater risk in the smaller towns – if Cricklewood's dairy factory closes, the town's property is likely to fall in value. The second is that capital growth in good locations is tax free and is also certain to be accompanied by rental growth.

A few people may aim for high-income/low-growth properties because they need that income to fund borrowings or because they are not working. However, this is usually short-sighted. These high-yield/low- (or no-) growth properties will at best stay as they are and within a few years even their income may be outstripped by their high-growth counterparts.

Finally, a note about the amount of time involved and the interpersonal skill that is required for successful property investment. While it is true that both of these are usually high, it does not have to be so. Much of the time involved in property (and a considerable amount of the interpersonal skill) is required to manage the properties once they have been purchased. Dealing with tenants and looking after properties is much more difficult (and for a much longer period of time) than the purchasing phase. Purchasing property takes only a few weeks – managing it can be for years. You can if you want alleviate this management chore by hiring someone to do it for you.

Even the purchasing phase, which often involves the cut-and-thrust of much negotiating and haggling, can be reduced. There are many successful property investors who do not negotiate at all. They assess what a property is worth to them and put in an offer – take it or leave it. These people are very disciplined – they know what is a good deal for them and won't buy if they can't get it. Some investors get a reputation for dealing in this way and real estate agents advise their vendors accordingly. If you operate like that when buying and have your properties managed for you, there is little need for any great interpersonal or negotiation skills.

SHARES

Like property, the features of shares can depend upon how you go about investing. Gearing (see **Secret 7**) will increase your capital growth and tax efficiency but decrease your cash income. Volatility/risk can be decreased somewhat by holding a wide portfolio of shares across several industries and decreased even further by owning shares in different countries. The time involved in shares and the skills required can also vary – some investors buy a spread of shares (or a passive index-tracking fund) and hold it unchanged for long periods of time; others however are far more active in buying and selling as they try to beat the index.

INTEREST-EARNING DEPOSITS

The benefits and characteristics of deposits may also vary a little. Some people buy and sell bonds quite frequently as they try to pick shifts in debt markets to their best advantage. This requires quite a lot of time and a great amount of skill – and perhaps a bit of luck! Similarly, you can increase your risk a degree or two if you want to chase higher returns with a small finance company. However, the chart (p. 52) is an accurate indicator of the average attributes of debt investing.

If you do not go through this matching process to fit your investments to your needs and personality, you are really just investing at random. Successful investment is about identifying a financial need and selecting the investment to fill that need. It is also about enjoyment (or at least not letting money and investment detract from your lifestyle). In the same way as you are unlikely to enjoy a pair of shoes that do not fit, you will not enjoy investments that aren't suitable. Chasing the highest return in an investment is a bit like picking a pair of shoes solely for their style and appearance. There are many other factors which in the long run are just as important.

Your position is your position. Your circumstances and personality are unlike everyone else's – you are unique. Therefore your investments should also be the same – unique to you.

SECRET 3

Buy for Yield – Capital Gain Will Look After Itself

▼ ▼ ▼ ▼

'By buying for income first, you are investing rather than speculating.'

N INVESTMENT TERMS, I AM A FUNDAMENTALIST. THAT means that I buy investments on the basis of their fundamental worth and their ability to generate income. This does not mean that capital gain is unimportant – clearly it is very important. But by buying for income first you are investing rather than speculating. By studying and analysing an investment's income, its sustainability and its likelihood for growth, you are far more likely to be successful than by simply guessing the future direction of the value of some asset.

It is this income (the yield) that drives your investments and actually gives them their value. An investment must carry a cash return, one that is not based on the change of its value (capital gain). This yield is profits and dividends (for shares), rentals (for property) and interest (for bonds and bank deposits). The cash yield from the investment is separate from the capital gain – but it does push up the value of the investment as it rises (or pulls it down as it falls).

Given that such income is the basic driver of investment value, it makes sense to assess and watch it first, confident that if you get that right you will also get the capital growth right.

> **Investments are valued by looking at the income that you can get from them.**

Investments are valued by looking at the income that you can get from them. The greater the income, the greater the amount which someone will pay for the investment. This principle is the same for all investments – shares, property and interest-earning deposits – although the terminology and arithmetic varies. However, the broad principle works like this:

$$\text{Value of Investment} = \frac{\text{income}}{\text{appropriate yield}} \times 100$$

As an example, taking a property with a rental income of $15,000 pa which should sell on a yield of 9%, the value would be:

$$\text{Value} = \frac{\$\,15,000}{9\%} \times 100 = \$166,666$$

This property should sell for $166,666.

Shares are no different in basic principle – if a company was paying a dividend of 35 cents for each share and most similar company shares sold at a dividend yield of 7%, the value of the shares would be

$$\text{Value} = \frac{35¢}{7\%} = 500¢$$

To value an investment is simple arithmetic. If you grow the income you will grow the capital value. Because investment is about income it is easy to calculate what you should pay for the investment. There are only two complicating factors:

▼ Finding out the amount of income.
▼ Finding out the appropriate yield.

INCOME

This can be very easy or very hard, depending upon what type of investment you are buying. For example, if you were going to buy an investment property, finding out the rent is easy – you ask the owner. If you are buying Government Stock, the income is well established. It is when you come to shares that difficulties can arise. It is easy enough to find out what a particular company's profit was last year, but more difficult to know what it is in the current year and what it will be in future years. This is also sometimes so with property. A rental property may have an existing rent which is above or below market – you will need to make an assessment of what the rent will be after it has been reviewed and take account of that accordingly.

> If you grow the income you will grow the capital value.

All investment is for the future – you buy an investment for its future income not the past income. The profits a company made in the past will be of some interest to you but the real question is what will it make in the future. At best, historic profits are only a useful pointer to likely future prospects.

To assess a company's future profits requires that you keep your ears and eyes open. Many sharebrokers make visits to companies to analyse their performance and estimate their future profits and then publish what they find. Some tip sheets and newspapers average all of the brokers' guesstimates and publish their findings. Sometimes directors of companies will tell the business news media what they are expecting to earn in the next year. Air New Zealand, for example, in announcing its result in 1997 said that it expected to make $200 million for the next year. This allows you to establish valuations very easily.

Nevertheless, careful analysis is often to no avail as companies can surprise (both pleasantly and unpleasantly) the market. (Air New Zealand later amended its profit projection to $150 million.) This is simply because of the very uncertain nature of business and is what makes shares difficult as investments.

APPROPRIATE YIELD

The yield which is appropriate for a particular investment is one of the most difficult things for new or inexperienced investors to grasp. Why, they ask, should one investment be valued at a 6% yield, another at a 9% yield and yet another at an 11% yield? How does this work? Who sets these yields?

To answer the last question first – the market in any particular investment area sets yields. The market in its buying and selling decides what is an appropriate return for an investment. If you are an investor in that market, then the decisions that you make help establish what is a reasonable return for a particular property, share or bond; your buying and selling is a part of setting fair value in that market.

Investment markets usually have lots of buyers and lots of sellers. There are people constantly studying and analysing various investments. Many such people are full-time professionals and they know what the prospects for a particular investment are compared to the prospects of another one. Over time the market decides that one type of investment deserves a yield of 6% while another should have a yield of 9%. It does this in the continuous process of buying and selling and on the basis of the security of the investment and its future prospects.

The market demands a higher yield from what it perceives as a poorer investment – that is, it is saying that if you want me to invest in this poorer security, I will want a higher initial return. The only adjustment that it can make to get that higher yield is to set a lower price. Given that the income is set, the only variable then is the price – buyers will stay out of the market until sellers are willing to sell at a price which gives a satisfactory yield.

For example, two banks decide to raise some money by selling some bonds. One bank is Banque Suisse of Zurich while the other is the lesser known (and somewhat less stable) Cricklewood Savings Bank. Both banks issue bonds which pay $10,000 pa of interest. Investors are in effect buying an income stream (in this case of $10,000 pa) and need to decide how much they are prepared to pay for that income.

Prudent investors will look at the two issuing institutions and no doubt will say that the Banque Suisse bonds are a better, more secure investment. Because of that they are prepared to accept a lower yield. All things considered, investors may in this case accept a 6% yield from Banque Suisse.

Investors would assess the Cricklewood Savings Bank quite differently. If they are to be persuaded to invest in those bonds they require a considerably higher return – perhaps 9%.

The comparison would look like this:

	Banque Suisse	Cricklewood Savings Bank
Annual income	$10,000	$10,000
Appropriate yield	6%	9%
Value of bond	$166,666	$111,111

The important thing to note is that because the annual income cannot be altered, the only thing that can be changed to get a higher or lower yield is the value or price of the investment.

Prudent investors will pay a price for an income stream.

All investment markets work like this. Prudent investors will pay a price for an income stream from an investment which will give them the yield that they seek. If they cannot get that yield they don't buy that investment. When that happens an investor is saying that this particular investment is too expensive and that they can do better elsewhere. If sufficient investors do that, there will be no buyers and so the price will have to fall until investors are attracted to buy.

There are two overriding factors which investors look at to decide the appropriate yield:

▼ **How sustainable is the profit from the investment?**
▼ **Is the profit likely to grow at all in the future?**

There will be different attributes amongst the three investment types which contribute to the above, but it is primarily the sustainability (or security) of investment profit and the probability of growth which establishes the yield (and therefore the price) of an investment.

Given then that investors (as opposed to speculators) value their investments by their income, what drives up the value of investments? There can be only two factors:

▼ **A rise in income.**
▼ **A fall in the yield which is required by the market.**

Only these factors can cause a rise in the value of your investments. If you want your investments to perform, you need to find ones which will either increase their income or be re-rated by the market to a lower yield because the market recognises that their income has become more secure or is likely to grow.

▼ SPECIAL NOTE: SECURITY OF INCOME

A small industrial property in Christchurch was rented to a very good tenant (a subsidiary of a big multinational corporation) for $17,500 pa. The lease had 1 year left to run at which point the tenant had a right of renewal for a further 6 years.

The owner needed to sell and approached some real estate agents. Their advice was to see if the tenant could be induced to renew the lease early. The owner went to the tenant who replied that no, they would not renew early.

So the owner put the property on the market with one year left on the lease (poor security of income for any purchaser). After advice, the property was listed at $160,000, representing an 11% yield for a new owner. This quite high yield (and low price) reflected the tenuous, short-term lease. However, even at that price there were no buyers, not even an offer.

After 6 months the owner withdrew the property from the market. As the time for the lease expiry drew near, the owner again approached the tenant – did they want to renew the lease? After a few weeks the tenant responded – yes, they would renew the lease for a further 6 years at the same rental.

Now the owner really had something to sell – a building with a brand-new lease to a multinational corporation. The owner put the building up for auction and in spirited bidding the property sold for $185,000 – a 9.5% yield.

The difference between no takers at $160,000 and an easy sale at $185,000 can be attributed to one thing – the renewal of the lease. That change in value was solely caused by the fact that an investor buying the building now had a good sustainable income.

Sometimes both happen – income rises, the market notices this and decides that this type of share or this type of property is so good that it deserves a lower yield. When that occurs, investors really make money.

One of the reasons that yields rise or fall is that the three investment types actually compete against each other. This means that investors, in their continual study of the prospects of different investments, will at various times rate one class of investment higher than others. For example, as they see the future prospects of, say, commercial property looking better and better, money will come out of bonds and out of equities and go into commercial property. As the money comes out of bonds and out of shares the price of those investments will fall and as they fall, their yields will rise. Likewise as the money goes into commercial property the price of that investment rises and so the yields fall. The higher yields now offered by bonds and shares become more attractive and so some investment money goes back to them. It is like a seesaw, always trying to find equilibrium but never really managing to (or not for long, anyway). This continual process is the nature of free and open markets.

The three investment types actually compete against each other.

The important thing for the new investor to recognise is that this is all income-driven. The values and prices of investments shift with the prospect of higher income and better yields.

While all investments are valued by their income, each of the three has different ways of expressing it. This may seem designed to confuse. However, provided you always keep in mind that it is the relationship between annual income and the value of the investment that is important, much of that confusion will disappear.

Here's how the three important types are valued:

VALUING PROPERTY

This is usually the most straightforward investment type to value. Property investors assess the net annual rental and compare that to the value as a percentage to get the yield.

$$\textbf{Property yield} = \frac{\textbf{net rental}}{\textbf{cost}} \times \textbf{100}$$

For example, a property with an annual income of $20,000 which has been purchased for $220,000 would have a yield of 9%.

$$\textbf{Property yield} = \frac{\textbf{\$20,000}}{\textbf{\$220,000}} \times \textbf{100} = \textbf{9\%}$$

There are two important things to note here:

▼ **In property, it is always the net yield that is important.** The net yield is calculated from the income after expenses such as rates, insurance and maintenance. These items need to be deducted from the gross rentals before doing your calculations.

▼ **The yield is calculated as if there were no borrowings on the property.** It is true that most property investors borrow to purchase their properties. However, so that you can fairly compare the value and returns of one property with another you must do your calculation as if there were to be no borrowing.

In property, it is always the net yield that is important.

This calculation can be reversed to value a property. You can value a property if you know what the rental is and what an appropriate yield should be:

$$\textbf{Property value} = \frac{\textbf{net rental}}{\textbf{appropriate yield}} \times \textbf{100}$$

For example, you have found a property with a net rental income of $25,000 pa and you believe that 9% would be a fair and appropriate return:

$$\text{Property value} = \frac{\$\,25,000}{9} \times 100 = \$277,777$$

If, however, you thought that the property was not very 'good' (ie, it is in Cricklewood, see **Secret 6**), you might decide that you need an 11% return to entice you to buy it:

$$\text{Property value} = \frac{\$\,25,000}{11} \times 100 = \$227,272$$

The difficult thing for some people to grasp is that the higher the yield, the lower the price – and vice versa. To buy in Cricklewood, you must get a higher cash yield than what you could get in Tauranga. The best way to think of it is that if you are assessing the property as of poorer quality you need a higher cash return from the rentals to be encouraged to buy it. The only variable that you can alter to get that higher yield is the price (or value) of the property.

The higher the yield, the lower the price – and vice versa.

The yields for good quality property usually stay within a reasonably narrow band for long periods of time. For example, Auckland industrial property usually trades at yields between 8.5% and 10%, Christchurch industrial property from 9.5% to 11%, etc. Occasionally they will move out of these bands but never for very long. When they do, they are probably indicating a very good time to buy or sell (as the case may be).

In the boom times of the mid 1980s, before the Crash, some office building yields went as low as 5% (instead of their more usual 8%), in spite of very high interest rates as a frenzied market bid up prices. Very high rental growth had attracted the market but after the Crash rentals actually fell considerably and yields rose to take account of the lack of growth. Although that market is now showing growth, values have yet to recover their levels of a decade ago.

VALUING SHARES

Shares are a bit more difficult. Shares are valued by their income but the complicating factor is that companies do not pay out all of their profits to shareholders. Most companies pay out around 40% of their profits to their shareholders by way of dividends and retain the rest to fund the growth of their operations. This percentage does vary, some paying out a large proportion of their profits to shareholders, others a very small amount. For example, GPG pays out only around 10% of its profits in dividends to shareholders (keeping the rest itself to buy new assets), while Telecom pays out nearly all (90%) of its profits.

The other complicating factor in understanding share valuations is the jargon and terminology. The most common and important comparison of a company's profit to its value is not often expressed as a percentage (like a yield); instead it is expressed as a ratio. This is called a Price:Earnings ratio.

When an expert share analyst goes into a company to assess its worth and prospects, they will look at a vast number of financial indicators, percentages and ratios. They will look at the stock turn, the quick ratio, equity ratio, market share, aged debtors, return on capital employed, amortisation rates . . . All of these things (and many more) are necessary for a full analysis of a company.

However, as a private investor, there are really only three major indicators that you need to be concerned with. They are:

▼ Price:Earnings ratio
▼ Dividend yield
▼ Net tangible assets ratio

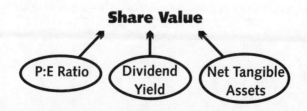

PRICE:EARNINGS RATIO

This is the most important indicator of a company's value – and it is much simpler than it sounds!

The ratio compares the earnings (or profits) of a company to its price or value. It is not a percentage, but the number of times the price is greater than the annual earnings. Put another way, it is the number of years that these profits would need to be made to equate to the price.

Imagine that a company has total profits of $250,000 pa after tax and it is to be sold for $2.0 million. What is the P:E ratio?

$$P:E = \frac{\$2,000,000}{\$250,000} = 8$$

This company has sold at 8 times its annual earnings.

However, few of us want to (or at least are able to) buy whole companies. What we do is buy a share (or a few shares) in a company. Therefore, rather than base our calculations on what the entire company is earning and what it is worth, we split it down so that we know what each share is earning (the earnings per share or eps) and what each share is worth.

Imagine that the above company had 400,000 shares on issue. The earnings per share (eps) would be:

$$eps = \frac{earnings}{shares\ on\ issue} = \frac{\$250,000}{400,000} = 62.5¢$$

If the P:E ratio of 8 is appropriate, the share price would be:

$$62.5¢ \times 8 = 500¢ \text{ or } \$5$$

This P:E allows you to easily compare the amount of earnings as it relates to the share price between companies. Similar companies in similar industries should have broadly similar P:E ratios.

EXAMPLE: MICHAEL HILL JEWELLERS AND HALLENSTEIN GLASSONS

Michael Hill Jewellers

Shares on issue: 39 million
Profit $5.1 million
Earnings per share   13 cents per share
Current share price   165¢

$$P:E \text{ ratio} = \frac{\textbf{share price}}{\textbf{earnings per share}} = \frac{165¢}{13¢} = 12.7$$

Hallenstein Glassons

Shares on issue: 58 million
Profit $11.2 million
Earnings per share   19 cents per share
Current share price   240¢

$$P:E \text{ ratio} = \frac{\textbf{share price}}{\textbf{earnings per share}} = \frac{240¢}{19¢} = 12.6$$

These broadly similar retail companies are very similarly priced compared to the profits that they are making. What the market was saying at this time was that both companies had similar prospects.

> **This is what sharemarket investors are looking for: companies which have a lower P:E than is warranted.**

Frequently, however, in the sharemarket you will find companies have widely differing P:E ratios – one will have a P:E ratio of say 9, while another will have one of 15. This may mean that the company which is cheaper compared to its earnings (the one trading on a P:E of 9) has poorer prospects. However, it may also be that the market has overlooked that company and it is a bargain. This is what sharemarket investors are looking for: companies which have a lower P:E than is warranted. Sooner or later the market will see that here is an opportunity to buy very cheap earnings. Provided that you are right and there is no reason for the company to be so cheap (you must always look in the mouth of gift horses) the market will one day re-rate the company, its P:E will rise as the share price is pushed up.

▼ SPECIAL NOTE: EARNINGS YIELD

The earnings yield is the inverse of the P:E ratio. It is calculated by comparing the share price to the total amount of profit, regardless of what happens to that profit – whether it is paid out in dividends or retained by the company. The earnings yield will differ from the dividend yield by the amount which is paid out in dividends.

Take a company which has 50 million shares on issue and which is making $6 million profit (or earnings) per annum. The earnings per share is 12 cents per share ($6m ÷ 50m = 12 cps). If the share price was 160¢, the earnings yield would be:

$$\text{earnings yield} = \frac{\text{eps}}{\text{share price}} \times 100 = \frac{12¢}{160¢} \times 100 = 7.5\%$$

The P:E ratio for the same company is 13.33. This figure (13.33) is the inverse of 7.5.

The earnings yield imagines that the company pays out all of its profits to shareholders in cash. If that did happen (and it seldom does) the earnings yield and the dividend yield would be the same.

Although the P:E ratio and the earnings yield measure and compare the same thing (ie, total earnings compared to share price), the P:E ratio is far more commonly used. In some ways that is a shame because it is a little harder for new share investors to understand.

The sharemarket does anticipate a company's future prospects and likely profits – after all, an investor is not buying a share of a company for last year's profits but for future years' profits. The stronger the likely growth in profit, the higher the P:E ratio, although of course the P:E ratio will fall as the profits rise.

This falling P:E ratio is very common – in fact any company which has profit growth will have lower prospective P:Es than historic ones. (A prospective P:E is based on future, budgeted, profit, rather than actual historic profit.)

Take as an example a company with 100 million shares on issue which is trading at 400¢. Last year its profit was $20 million but this is forecast to rise in the next two years to $25 million and $33 million. The figures would look like this:

Year	Profit	No of Shares	eps	P:E
1998	$20 million	100 million	20¢	20
1999	$25 million	100 million	25¢	16
2000	$33 million	100 million	33¢	12.1

As you can see, the P:E ratio is predicted to fall from 20 to 12.1 over 3 years as the profitability of the company increases. In fact, as long as the company's prospects remain good, the greater the likelihood that the share price will increase so that the P:E ratio remains at 20. The share price would increase like this:

Year	Profit	eps	P:E	Share price
1998	$20 million	20¢	20	400¢
1999	$25 million	25¢	20	500¢
2000	$33 million	33¢	20	666¢

You should not put your money into shares without knowing the profit that each share is going to get.

All that is really happening here is that the share price is going up with profitability.

Many small private investors will not want to do all the detailed analysis to estimate future profits themselves. There are a number of excellent publications which will do this for you and some sharebrokers publish their research and recommendations to clients. However, as a bare minimum you should understand P:E ratios and how they work before investing in the sharemarket. After all, the ratio is measuring what likely income will accrue to each share that you own. You would not put your money in the bank without knowing the interest rate – you should not put your money into shares without knowing the profit that each share is going to get.

DIVIDEND YIELD

The dividend yield is simply a measure of the cash dividend that you are likely to receive each year compared to the price that you have paid for the share. In this respect, it is a little like the interest rate you get from the bank – you put your money in and receive a cash return. It must be stressed again that most companies do not pay out all of their profits in dividends – they retain some, using it to repay debt, buy plant and equipment, etc. You of course as a shareholder still own a part of these retained profits (usually called 'retained earnings' in the company's accounts); it is just that you do not receive them in cash.

Most companies make two dividend payments each year – the interim dividend and the final dividend. Added together they give the total dividend which can then be compared to the share price to get the dividend yield:

Telecom
Interim dividend	10 cents per share
Final dividend	20 cents per share
Total dividend	**30 cents per share**

$$\text{Dividend yield} = \frac{\textbf{annual dividend}}{\textbf{share price}} \times 100 = \frac{30\text{¢}}{820\text{¢}} \times 100 = \textbf{3.66\%}$$

This means that if you purchased Telecom shares in that year at 820¢, you would get a cash return from dividends of 3.66%.

This may sound a little low (compared to what you get at the bank, for example) but you need to keep in mind two things:

▼ **Most dividends are 'fully imputed'; that is, tax has already been paid on them and they will be tax-free in your hands.** This means that the dividend pay-out is equivalent to 5.5% before tax.

▼ **The dividends are likely to grow as the company makes more profits.**

The dividend yield is not the most important guide to a company's performance because it does not measure the company's total profitability – it only compares the amount which is paid out to shareholders. However, it is important, especially for those who need income from their investments. Such investors will look for companies that pay out most of their profits. Companies such as Telecom can afford to do this because they have huge cashflows. Telecom has a tax-paid profit of $800m but it has a net cash income of $1400m. It can therefore afford to pay out its $800m profit to shareholders as dividends while using the balance ($600m) to fund expansion and new plant and equipment. The main difference between the cash income of $1400m and its tax-paid profit of $800m is that it can claim depreciation of $600m from its profit for tax purposes. All this makes Telecom good for investors who need income. Investors who do not need income usually look for companies like GPG who do not pay out much of their profits to shareholders but who hold onto them to grow the company.

> **Those investors who do not need income should be sure to re-invest their dividends.**

Those investors who do not need income, however, should be sure to re-invest their dividends (even when they are small), probably by taking shares in lieu of cash dividends. This is because of the compounding effect which means that you are getting dividends on dividends and this grows your wealth considerably over time.

NET TANGIBLE ASSETS RATIO

This measure has nothing to do with income but can provide a check to ensure that you are not paying too much goodwill for particular shares.

Net tangible assets are the value of the tangible assets (things like plant and equipment, land and buildings, cash, debtors and stock) less liabilities (trade creditors, bank borrowings). The net tangible assets are then divided by the number of shares on issue to give the net tangible assets per share. This is then compared to the share price.

For example, a company has 20 million shares on issue and the shares are trading at 94¢.

Tangible assets	**$35 million**
Less liabilities	**($21 million)**
Net tangible assets	**$14 million**

$$\text{Net tangible assets per share} = \frac{\text{nta}}{\text{shares on issue}} = \frac{\$14\,m}{20\,m} = 70¢$$

This means that while the shares are valued at 94¢ on the market, each share has 70¢ of tangible assets. The company is trading on the market at a premium over nta of 24¢ – ie, the market value of the shares is 24¢ greater than the value of the tangible assets. This extra premium is goodwill and the market is prepared to pay that because the company is using its assets efficiently to make good profits. Sometimes, however, companies trade at a discount to their net tangible assets – this would mean that the net tangible assets would be say 70¢ per share while the shares are trading at 40¢. This is an asset stripper's dream. An asset stripper would try to buy the whole company at 40¢, and sell off the businesses or the assets, all at a handsome profit. (It may also see you as a shareholder make a good profit too as the asset stripper needs to bid up the share price to get complete control.)

Net tangible asset backing has most relevance in the event of insolvency or break-up of the company. If that happens a high net tangible asset backing will mean that not only will all of the banks and creditors get paid, but so too the shareholders.

Net tangible assets is the least important share valuation item. As an investor, I care little about it, being far more concerned with the sustainable income and earnings of the company. Telecom, for example, does not have a very high net tangible asset backing but it has great cashflow and good strong (and growing) earnings (or profits).

INTEREST-BEARING DEPOSITS

Many interest bearing deposits do not need to be valued – you put your money in the bank, you get interest, and you take it out when you want it. Such deposits cannot be traded so you do not need to value them.

However, some deposits do trade. There are markets for money just as there are markets for shares and property. They are called the money markets.

The money markets trade such things as Bank Bills, Treasury Bills and Commercial Bills. Most of these are traded on the wholesale market (ie, they are very large sums of money) and are therefore of fairly limited interest to most smaller private investors. However, one area of more interest to private investors are bonds. These are such things as Government Stock, Local Authority Stock or bonds issued by corporations such as Electrocorp, Telecom, or the port companies.

Most bonds are long-dated, that is they are usually for periods of 3 to 10 years (in the USA some Government bonds are for 30 years). A bond will pay a fixed rate of interest until maturity. The interest rate paid will depend on the creditworthiness of the issuer – so bonds issued by the New Zealand Government will have a lower interest rate than those issued by a State Owned Enterprise, which will be lower again than bonds issued by a smaller privately owned corporate.

An investor might hand over $50,000 to the New Zealand Government and get a piece of paper promising to pay the $50,000 back in 10 years and pay 7% interest in the meantime. You would think that would be the end of it. But it isn't!

There is in New Zealand a very busy secondary market for bonds, which are constantly bought and sold. So even though you have bought your bond from the Government for ten years, you can sell it to another investor before the maturity date.

As with other investments, you may make a capital profit or loss on this transaction. Interest rates fluctuate continually and depending on which way they move you could sell your paper to another investor for more or less than what you paid for it.

Imagine that you have purchased a $10,000 bond at 7.5%. If after two years you wanted (or needed) to sell it, an investor will pay an amount to reflect the prevailing interest rate at the time. That investor does not care what you paid for the bond – all she cares about is receiving the interest rate that prevails in the market at the time.

Because the income of your bond is fixed, the only way the buyer can get the market interest rate is to alter the capital sum. Therefore if rates have risen, she will offer less than the $10,000 you paid – perhaps $9500. If interest rates have fallen she will pay more, maybe $10,500, giving you a capital gain on the transaction. (You should note that this gain is not tax-free as most capital gains are in New Zealand. The $500 profit that you have made is taxable.)

There are people who spend their time trying to trade bonds in this way to make a profit. They buy when interest rates are high and then sell when they are low. It is an activity fraught with difficulty – interest rates change because of all sorts of factors: political activity, Reserve Bank moves, inflation, overseas events, economic activity, etc.

The actual calculation to value bonds at different interest rates is quite difficult and involves such variables as the coupon (or original) rate, maturity date, current interest rate, next interest payment due date, etc. Some bonds of course will change hands many times over the five or ten years of their life as just like shares they are bought and sold by different people. The important thing to recognise is that like all investments, they are valued by the income that can be derived from them.

Of course some investors buy bonds and never trade them. These are people who need a set amount of income for a long period of time. They do not want to put their money in the bank for say 6 months because when that deposit matures and they want to roll it over, they might find that interest rates have fallen and their income will fall with it. Most wise investors will have some bonds in their portfolios to hedge against a fall in interest rates.

Never forget that not all bonds are created equal!

However, never forget that not all bonds are created equal! Skellerup (a medium-sized New Zealand company) issued bonds to investors at a 10% interest rate. As the company teetered on the brink of collapse the price of these bonds fell as bond holders offered up to a 100% interest rate to quit them. In the USA, bonds issued by smaller corporations which have a lot of borrowings are called 'junk bonds' – a good name! The Skellerup bonds turned out to be fairly junky.

No longer can you buy shares on the basis of a tip from your sister-in-law or buy any old property because 'property always goes up in value and they're not making any more' – markets and the participants in them are too sophisticated for that. This is your money that you are investing – it may have been hard-earned! In any case it should work hard for you. That means buying investments on the basis of their intrinsic worth and what they can earn. It does not mean speculating with things which have no worth other than the hope that someone will come along behind you and pay more for them than you did.

You should buy investments with good sustainable (and growing) income. If you keep to that, the capital gains will follow!

SECRET 4

Markets Act, React and Over-React

▼ ▼ ▼ ▼

'A market is a big continuous debate.'

D AVID LANGE ONCE SAID THAT MARKET BEHAVIOUR is like that of reef fish. The description is apt – all seems calm and quiet with everyone going about their business when suddenly a shadow passes over. Thinking it might be a shark, all the players rush somewhere else where they return to their calm ways (for a time at least). Now that they are in their new place they do not care that the shadow was not in fact a shark but the sun going behind a very small cloud.

David Lange's quip is amusing and shows considerable insight into how markets act, react and over-react. An understanding of how markets behave is important to investors. Just as important is knowing why they act as they do and what you can do about it.

A market is a big continuous debate. Like a debate, there are two sides, each opposing the other. With a debate, one side is the negative while the other is the affirmative – with a market, one is buying, one is selling. The buyers in the market are the bulls (they toss the market up with their horns) while the sellers are commonly called bears (they try to claw the market down). Market debates are ultimately scored with money – investors putting their money in, or pulling it out.

Two opposing opinions are an absolute necessity to create a market; there must be doubt and uncertainty. If there is not, the market will immediately move to a point where the two sides are again basically in balance. Like a debate, the two sides need to be roughly of equal strength. There is no fun in any debate where one side has a far easier proposition to put or defend. Similarly, a market cannot exist if there are not both buyers and sellers, bulls and bears, in roughly equal numbers and strength. In fact, if you are an investor looking for valuable assets (preferably at a discount) uncertainty is your friend. Without uncertainty there would simply be no one to sell you a good value investment.

Any expert debater is able to make both cases equally well – she could argue for the affirmative just as convincingly as she could argue the negative. Good investors should be able to do the same – they should be able to say why they should sell an investment just as well as they can give their reasons for buying one. It has to be realised and acknowledged that the person who is selling you an investment is doing so for a reason. Certainly there will be some sellers who are simply following along with everyone else or perhaps because they need the cash – but there will be others who have carefully considered the market and their investments within it and have decided to sell. Not all reef fish are stupid!

Both sides have good reasons for their actions – if they did not, no market would exist.

Both sides of any market, the buyer and the seller, have their reasons for acting. As an astute, principled investor you should be able to state both sides of the argument as a check on your own position. If you make the case for both sides you will be able to choose readily and easily which of the sides you want to be on. One or other side will ultimately be more convincing to you and cause you to act one way or the other. However, always remember that both sides have good reasons for their actions – if they did not, no market would exist.

▼ SPECIAL NOTE: UNCERTAINTY RULES

In mid 1997 I bought some Air NZ shares at around 280¢. Air NZ's profit had fallen from $225m (1996) to $150m (1997) but the company had announced moves to reverse that decline. My reasons for buying were:

1. The company had announced a cost-saving programme that would save $100m a year and bring the profit to around $200m.
2. At that profitability Air NZ was on a P:E of around 8 and a dividend yield of over 10%.
3. The Sydney Olympics, Millenium events and America's Cup were likely to increase tourism in the next few years.

All went well with the investment for a few weeks as the share price rose to about 310¢.

Then economic turmoil hit Asia. The New Zealand sharemarket looked around for companies which would be adversely affected by this and decided that Air NZ flew into Asia, that much of New Zealand's tourism was from Asia and that Air NZ would not be able to keep to its $200m projected profit. The reef fish scattered and the share price dropped to 210¢. This was more than a little alarming to me – there were compelling reasons for the fall – so I considered cutting my losses and selling.

However, before I did I checked out the reality of the situation. After some time on the phone to a couple of brokers I started to realise that in fact Asia was a fairly small part of Air NZ's business. Then Air NZ itself announced that it was aiming for a profit of $150m, causing the price to drop further to 200¢.

I did some more arithmetic – at 200¢ the P:E ratio was down to about 6 and the dividend yield was over 13%. It was good investment at those levels, so instead of selling I decided to hold on.

There were sound reasons for the market selling Air NZ down – but also good reasons for buying into it. Time will tell which course of action was right.

Markets always over-react, on both the upside and the downside. By this I mean markets will usually go to a point further than what the majority of players would expect or perhaps even want. When a market runs up (a bull market), values go higher than what is warranted; and when they go down (a bear market), they go below their true worth. Markets nearly always over-react like this as they struggle vainly to find equilibrium.

The reason that markets behave like this is that markets are driven by emotion. The emotions which move markets are greed on the upside and fear on the downside. While it would be comforting to believe that all people in the market are making their decision logically and behaving rationally, in fact they often are not – many are driven by fear and greed.

These emotions at times cause people to lose sight of what they are actually doing. Greed creates a frenzy of buying,

> **Greed creates a frenzy of buying, while fear creates a frenzy of selling.**

while fear creates a frenzy of selling. In the stampede, people care little about values and analysis – all they care about is that they are in or they are out (as the case may be) as fast as possible.

People and markets often feed off their own success. People make investments and the investments go up in value: this rewards their behaviour so they put more money in which pushes the market even higher. This cycle, explicable in terms of behavioural psychology, was surely a large factor in the big bull run on both the share and property markets in New Zealand in the 1980s. The continual reward for the behaviour of investments led to more money going in with a result of overvalued markets.

This phenomenon is exacerbated by the fact that markets anticipate or work ahead of themselves. In investing, you are looking forward to future profits and income from your investments. Because of this, anything which happens or is announced now will immediately be factored into the price today. Good news which is likely to see greater earnings or rentals in the future is reflected immediately in the share price. In fact, the sharemarket tends to be about 6-9 months in front of the economy in general. If the economy is strong but the sharemarket is tracking down, that is usually because the sharemarket is expecting the economy to weaken. This means the sharemarket is usually a very accurate barometer of the economy. Just as a barometer can help predict the weather, so can the sharemarket help predict the direction of the economy. (The sharemarket is also a very good pointer to what is likely to happen at election time. Watching the sharemarket is usually far more useful in picking election results than watching opinion polls.)

However, markets do often get their expectation wrong – they over-anticipate (and therefore over-react). This is the root of that old sharemarket saying: 'Buy the rumour and sell the fact.' It means that the market will factor into the price the rumour of something good happening and therefore the price does not move when (or if) the rumour becomes a public announcement. Sometimes if there are no rumours, the public announcement of, say, a purchase, pushes up the price but when the purchase is made the share price settles back to more realistic levels.

▼ SPECIAL NOTE: MEET THE MARKET

In the final analysis the market is always right. This may not be true in the short term (where the market may be undervalued or overvalued for a little while) but in the long term the market sets fair value.

Although you need to be a principled investor who acts on the basis of your personal assessment of value, you do need to meet the market. There have been many people, both buyers and sellers, who have regretted waiting for the market to make some small adjustment to meet their value assessment. More important than buying or selling at your own precise valuation is that you are in or out of the market (as the case may be).

When I buy or sell shares, I ask my broker for the quotes. While I am on the phone, I put in my buy price and see the deal done then and there. This may mean that I buy at 397¢ (instead of 395¢) but in the scheme of things I do not believe that 2¢ is likely to make much difference. I have seen too many people trying to save 2¢ and who have missed out completely as the shares run up and don't stop till they hit 500¢.

Similarly I have seen property sellers reject offers of $500,000 because they are $5,000 or $10,000 too low. If those offers are the best available (and in real estate your first offer is usually your best offer), then you need to decide whether you are going to meet the market and sell, or not. There seems no point in holding out against the market for a relatively small amount. If you don't meet the market, the market is likely to leave you behind.

In fact, the Efficient Market Theory says that an efficient market is one where prices already reflect all known information. If a market is truly efficient you should be able to select any bond, share or property at random and find that it is properly priced. Although clearly our markets have a degree of efficiency, they are not fully efficient. There are bargains available – ie, investments which are not fully priced – especially in the property and equity markets.

Markets are not always properly valued (in the short term) because it is people (with all of their foibles) who are making the buy/sell decisions. These are frequently made emotionally, on the spur of the moment and with little thought. For example, someone buys an investment property for $120,000. A few months later he is approached by someone wishing to buy it for $140,000. Thinking of the $20,000 profit he has made in such a short time he agrees to sell. Now he has to find something else to do with his money, requiring time, energy and cost. What he should have realised is that if the property had risen that much he was onto a winner and let his profits run. By selling he wasn't really making a profit, just crystallising the profit he had already made.

> **Purchase price is absolutely irrelevant – it should not be a factor in any sell decision.**

Similar situations happen frequently on the sharemarket. An investor buys some shares at 200¢. They go up in value to 260¢. Delighted with her 30% profit she sells, congratulating herself (and celebrating) but ignoring the fact that these shares keep on running upwards for months or even years. On the other hand, the shares fall in value to 150¢. Annoyed she decides to sell – but only when they have gone back to 200¢, when she has got her money back. That may be in months, years or never – the shares have not fallen 50¢ for no reason at all and she needs to look for that reason to see if it is serious. In fact purchase price is absolutely irrelevant – it should not be a factor in any sell decision.

Neither response to the shares going up or down (nor the response to the unsolicited offer for the property) is sensible or rational. The responses are at variance with that old market adage that you should cut your losses but let your profits run. The main point is that none of these responses is a thinking approach, made after careful consideration. They are responses made on emotion – delight at a price rise, annoyance at a fall.

TWO MARKET THEORY

As an investor you need to be aware that often there are two markets of importance for the investments that you hold. One of these markets is about the capital value of your investment (the buy/sell market), while the other is the market which dictates the income from the investment. For example, property investors need to study the market which shows the price at which properties are being bought and sold, but they also need to watch the leasing market, the value or price that rentals are set at.

Of these two, the market which sets the income from an investment is more important in the long run than the buy/sell market. Over long periods of time, yields and P:E ratios tend to stay in a fairly narrow band. Only occasionally, in times which are for some reason quite extraordinary, do these value-setters (P:E ratios and yields) move greatly outside of these bands. They do in fact remain relatively constant over long periods of time. It is not a major fall in P:E ratios or property yields that has caused property and equity markets to rise over the decades. It is in fact increasing profits and increasing rentals which has fuelled that rise.

This is less so over shorter terms (say less than five years). During these periods, a change in the return that investors expect or demand might account for perhaps 20-30%, as yields move from 9% to 11% or P:E ratios from 16 to 18. Clearly it is possible to benefit from these.

However, over long periods of time it is the increase in income that pushes up markets. Therefore the market that is more important is the one that dictates a rise or a fall in that income.

PROPERTY

I have long believed that wise property investors should study the 'For Lease' columns of their daily papers much more carefully than they study the 'For Sale' columns. Clearly what they are looking for are areas where there is more demand by renters (whether residen–tial or commercial) than there is supply. The astute property investor is constantly looking for areas where there will be rental growth.

I have long believed that wise property investors should study the 'For Lease' columns of their daily papers.

This is the reason that location is so important in property investment. A good location is simply one where people will want to rent. In such a location, the demand for space is such that supply cannot keep up, thus driving up rentals and values. Sometimes such locations are limited in size in some way – the area is hemmed in and cannot be expanded to meet demand.

▼SPECIAL NOTE: LOOK TWICE

Property purchasers should look at their prospective acquisition at least twice and at different times of the day. Beware going back for a second look at the same time of day as the first look. If you do that you will see the same property in the same conditions.

Go back for your second look when the light, sun and wind are different from the first time. The property will not appear the same – maybe better, maybe worse, maybe just different.

For example, the area of Sydenham in Christchurch has long been fruitful for industrial property investors. Sydenham is close to the city and major arterial routes (both road and rail) and is therefore very convenient for many business people. However, Sydenham is locked in by the central city on one side and residential houses on the other – it cannot be enlarged, since the amount of space available is strictly limited. If you compare the rents in Sydenham to those in Bromley (another Christchurch industrial area but one that has huge amounts of bare land which can be built on), you will find that the rents in Bromley are less than half of those in Sydenham. Property investors in Sydenham have been rewarded correspondingly.

SHARES

The income of companies comes from the businesses that they run. Astute sharemarket investors are watching company profitability more than anything else. No one should ever invest in a company without understanding the company's business, how it actually makes its money. It is true of course that companies can be re-rated by the sharemarket (a struggling company might restructure its business to better secure its profits and therefore be re-rated by the market from a P:E of, say, 8 to a P:E of 12). However, most long-term share price growth comes from growth in profits.

Sharemarket investors need to watch three things: the economy (or economies) that their investment operates in, the industry that the company competes in and the company itself. Because the first two of these are more important, it is probably useful to think of it as a triangle.

No one should ever invest in a company without understanding the company's business.

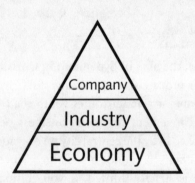

The economy overall is the base; the market or industry sits on that base and the individual company sits on that. This is not to say that company cannot operate well in a poor economy or in an industry which is struggling. Some can do well regardless of the economic or industry climate, but not many. It is so much harder and management needs to be so much better.

For example, imagine the operation of The Warehouse, a New Zealand retailer. If the economy was in recession or if retail trade was doing badly, that company would need to work very hard to maintain let alone increase its profits. To outperform an industry or the economy generally comes down to strength of management.

Sharemarket investors look at these three things, continually assessing and reassessing them. They pick up on any snippet of gossip, like reef fish darting off away from any dark cloud, or rushing towards anything that reef fish favour. They are looking at the strength of the economy, how particular industries are performing within the economy and the abilities of management. An investor considering The Warehouse would assess the New Zealand economy (the only place that the company operates so far), looking at such factors as exchange rates, interest rates, growth, political factors, unemployment, etc. She would then study the retail industry, taking account of any expected tax cuts (or rises), amount of competition, and trends in retail sales. Finally she assesses the company itself, where it sits in the market, where it gets it stock from, its competitive advantage, future plans (expansion to Australia?) and, most importantly, its management abilities. Ultimately she is trying to understand The Warehouse's business, determining whether people are likely to shop and buy there in greater or lesser numbers.

All of these things will make up the company's ability to generate increased profits and therefore show increased dividends and share price. They are harder to assess and monitor than the sharemarket itself. It requires some business, financial and even economic skill and knowledge. Such assessment is important and regardless of how difficult it is, it needs to be done and done well.

INTEREST-EARNING DEPOSITS

The amount of interest that particular deposits attract can vary greatly over time. It was not so very long ago (perhaps 10 years) that you could get 30% on bank bills (instead of the current 8%). This matters little for short-term investors as their deposits roll over every few weeks or months and so they are usually never very far away from receiving the market interest rate. However, it makes a great deal of difference to those who invest in long-dated fixed-interest bonds. These people may be purchasing an investment with a fixed rate of interest for as long as 10 years. If the debt markets move, they are a long way from getting a market interest rate unless they sell up their bonds, possibly taking a capital loss. And of course rates are almost certain to move substantially over that period of time.

YIELD CURVE

Most serious investors study the 'yield curve' very closely. The yield curve is a graph which plots the different rates of interest available, depending upon the term that you invest for. So, a financial institution may offer 6% for money on call, 6.5% for a 2-month investment and 6.75% for a 6-month investment.

There are both positive yield curves and negative yield curves. A positive yield curve means that the longer the investment, the higher the rate of interest. A negative yield curve means that the longer the period the lower the interest rate.

A positive yield curve looks like this:

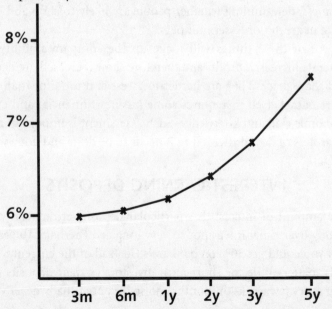

A positive yield curve is most usual. Investors are in effect demanding (and getting) a higher interest rate for long-term money because there is at least some risk (if not expectation) of higher interest rates in the future. Investors want and need to be compensated for the risk of tying up their money for the long term by receiving a higher rate of interest.

A negative (or inverse) yield curve looks like this:

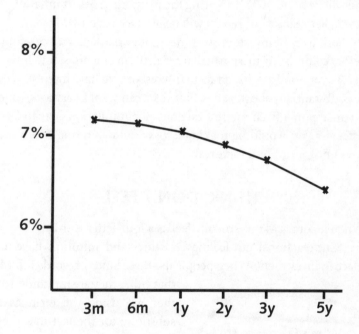

A yield curve of this shape usually means that there is a market expectation that interest rates will fall. Investors are wanting to lock in what they see as a good rate for as long as possible. Money therefore has gone into long-date securities, pushing down their rates.

Although a positive yield curve is usually the norm, in recent times New Zealand has frequently had a negative yield curve. This is due to tight monetary conditions and very low inflationary expectations. Serious debt investors (especially those who invest large sums and where small interest rate differences can mean a lot of money) take into account many economic factors before investing. In particular they watch the rate of inflation. This is because they are in no way hedged and covered for inflation if it happened to increase markedly. Investors in ownership assets (property and shares) are covered if inflation gets away – debt investors, especially those in long-term bond markets, are not.

Debt investors are most interested in their 'real rate of return'. This is the rate of return that they will get after taxation and inflation. For example, if an investor buys a bond yielding 7.5% she will be taxed at 33% to bring the net yield to 5%. If inflation is at 2%, her real rate of return will be 3% (see page 18).

Serious debt investors assess the money markets very carefully before committing to a particular term. It can be a disaster to invest in a 5-year bond at a fixed rate of interest only to have interest rates rise substantially shortly after. Five years can seem a very long time if you are on a fixed interest rate of 7% but inflation goes to 5%. After tax you would be making a loss – and counting down the days until your bond matures.

THINK, DON'T FEEL

When it comes to investment, 'feel' is a four-letter word.

'Gut reactions', 'gut feelings', 'instinct' and 'intuition' have no place in investment. When people use these kinds of words I think that either they are misguided or they are using the term as a substitute for the fact that they have analysed the investment in their mind without ever seeming to do so. There are undoubtedly some very astute and experienced investors who can do this,

> **When it comes to investment, 'feel' is a four-letter word.**

perhaps in their subconscious. Nevertheless, it is not good enough to buy an investment because you 'feel' it is going to be good.

Investment needs rational thought. It is a science, not an art, demanding careful judgement and discipline.

Most successful investors know what they are doing. More to the point, they know precisely why they are doing it. Whether buying or selling, a successful investor has scrutinised and analysed before she acts. Even in holding an investment she knows why she is holding it. A successful investor knows the market that she is in and the individual investments that she holds. She knows because she has studied them. She is likely to be able to tell you immediately everything that you would need to know about her investments – the P:E ratio or dividend yield for her shares and those for similar shares in her market; the rental and yield for her properties in that market; the interest rate and credit rating of the issuer for her bonds. If she cannot tell you these things off the top of her head she can easily go to her files and quickly look them up.

Successful investors are organised – they have information including annual reports, articles of interest, notes of conversations on file, readily available. Some investors may spend months researching particular investments or investment types. They may watch a company or a particular property type for some time, collecting information and analysing it before they make a move. In the case of a company, they may buy a few shares, following the company's progress before increasing their holdings.

All of this may seem difficult. It may be that it is too hard, in which case perhaps you are better to invest through managed funds or by buying into a range of investments spread across different types which will give you an average return. There is nothing wrong with this; it is perfectly reasonable. However, those who really want to succeed at investment and outperform the markets need to put in the work – there is no alternative. If it was easy, everyone would be doing it. To outperform, to beat the average, you need to be better informed, better organised and have better judgement.

Above all, you need to apply logic and reason. Much of the rest of the market is working instinctively and emotionally, driven by fear and greed. An ability to stand back from that, an ability to remove yourself from the whirl of the markets, is invaluable. This is not as easy as it sounds – no easier than being able to see a forest when you are in the midst of trees. It can be difficult to stay out of a market that is running upwards – difficult to sit on your hands even though you know logically that the market is over-reacting and going higher than it should. Even when you are sure that the market is behaving irrationally it is difficult not to get caught up in the hype and buy in.

That standing back can be a bit lonely. Everyone is invited to a party but you are not going. Always remember, however, that you are not going to the party because you are choosing to stay home; you have been invited but you don't want to go. Remember also that there will always be other good investment opportunities available – there always are. Just because you miss one good investment or bull run is no reason for despondency – there will be others. Too many people give up when they believe that they have missed out on an opportunity. They may have missed out on that opportunity but at any particular time, in any particular market, there is always at least one good opportunity. So you missed out on Brierley in 1962 and Broken Hill in 1968? So what? The succeeding years have continuously yielded others as good.

HAVE A PLAN

The easiest path to rational investment behaviour is to have a plan. A plan is like a filter – it allows the good through, while sorting out and stopping the rubbish. A plan allows you to find good investments which fit and suit your needs while rejecting the heavily promoted junk. When you work to a plan, investment decisions are easier – either it fits with your plan (in which case it gets more scrutiny and analysis) or it does not fit with your plan, in which case it is rejected out of hand.

> **A plan is like a filter – it allows the good through, while sorting out and stopping the rubbish.**

It would be interesting to know how many of the people who have purchased things like Gold Coast property, ostriches and 'investment plates' have had a plan and have made these investments because they fitted into the plan.

A plan allows you to stand back and remove yourself from the emotional noise of the markets. Planning is done at a quiet time. It is not done at a time when there is pressure to make a decision, nor when there are competing claims from the promoters of different investments. It is done calmly and rationally, without emotion.

Investment planning can be done on a number of levels and in a number of ways.

▼ **Stage in life.** There is a broad process through which most people should go. This is to purchase a house, repay the mortgage as quickly as possible, build a base of solid investments (probably a diversified portfolio) and then invest more aggressively.

Purchase House
↓
Repay Debt
↓
Solid Investments
↓
Aggressive Investments
↓
Capital Stable Investments

While not everyone will go through this process quite as neatly as that, it is a major well-formed path followed by many. You need to decide where you fit in that continuum and act accordingly. Age will also play a part in this planning process. Older people will tend to take less risks than younger people as they have less time to rectify their mistakes and restore their finances.

▼ **Diversification.** A conscious decision and plan is needed to establish the amount of diversification that is desirable. Clear, rational thought is needed to decide which markets you should be in and to what extent. Decisions regarding diversification and the particular markets to be in or out of revolve around the degree of risk that you are comfortable with, your investment skills and aptitudes and your interest in and enjoyment of particular investment types.

A plan dictating the type of markets you want to invest in is critical if you want to avoid being stampeded into dubious investments. A clear strategy to be in certain markets means that you will quickly reject 'opportunities' that do not figure.

▼ **Suitability.** This is the personal suitability process that helps you fit yourself to the correct investments, as outlined in Chapter 2.

▼ **Short-term planning.** There are often occasions when you need to map out what you are going to do over the next few weeks or months. Again, this needs to be done properly to ensure that there is no distraction or deviation. For example, like most investors I did not get enough of the giant Australian phone company Telstra when it floated in November 1997. The price on listing was well above the float price of 240¢ and just kept on going upwards. Even though the company seemed fully valued I was mindful of the performance of New Zealand's Telecom and that Telstra needed to be a core stock holding in any long-term portfolio. Worried that the market was overheating somewhat I decided to take the timing decision out of the equation by dollar cost averaging (see page 168). Each month for 6 months I would put the same amount of money into Telstra regardless of the price. I resolved to carry out this plan unless something of major significance happened to cause me to review it.

> **It helps greatly if you commit your investment plan to writing.**

It helps greatly if you commit your investment plan to writing. There is a discipline to a written plan which is not the same if you merely have a plan in your head, no matter how carefully it is thought out. A written plan is much more difficult to ignore (especially if it is made in conjunction with your partner) and much more difficult to deviate from. Not to carry out a written plan requires a very good reason.

Nevertheless there will be times when you do not follow the original plan that you have written – times when that reason is apparent. These might involve major changes either to your personal circumstance or to the circumstances within the markets. However, it is important to recognise that you do not deviate from your plan – you change the plan. This might seem a very fine distinction but it is an important one. To change what you intend to do cannot be done on a whim if you must first change your written plan. You are forced to go back and review the plan, to remember why it was set in the way it was.

The plan acts as a check.

For example, you have a diversified portfolio of investments including shares, property and some bonds. You are offered an investment property which is of such quality and of such a (low) price that you are very tempted. However, to buy it would mean selling some shares and/or some bonds (thus changing your planned asset allocation), or perhaps borrowing heavily (which is not in the plan). The plan now acts as a check – why did you have that asset allocation? How will it look if you change it? Why did you not want any debt? Why did you not have the search for bargain investments in the plan? If the plan was right then, how come it is not right now? Ultimately, you may decide to change your plan and buy the property, such is the attractiveness of the deal. On the other hand, you may decide to stay with the plan and either not buy the property or buy the property but plan to sell one of your other properties when you can, to keep your asset allocation as was decided. Only you, in full knowledge of your circumstances, can make this decision. A plan will at the very least make you aware of what all of those circumstances are and give you a cooling-off period to calmly and rationally reconsider.

SECRET 5

You Can Manage Risk

▼ ▼ ▼ ▼

*'Much of risk management
is about protecting the
downside while
advancing the upside.'*

THE FIRST RETURN SHOULD BE THE RETURN OF YOUR capital. This is a safety-first approach. Your investment is not a good one if you cannot get your capital when you need it.

I had a client once who telephoned me to tell me the wonderful investment he had just made. A small finance company was giving him 22% for 60 days call when banks were only giving 13-14%. But why, I asked, would they be giving you 22% if a bank is giving so much less? Within two weeks this finance company (Burberry Finance) had gone into liquidation. All of a sudden the 22% didn't seem very good any more.

> **The greatest risk comes from getting into things that you know little about.**

The relationship between high risk and high return may be clichéd but nevertheless it is true. If you are investing in something which is offering a higher return, there is likely to be higher risk unless of course you take steps to manage that risk. Probably the greatest risk comes from getting into things that you know little about. The reason that great investors succeed with apparently risky undiversified portfolios is that they know what they are doing. Someone with the knowledge and skill of a Warren Buffett or Sir Ronald Brierley can confidently take a position, backing himself to be right. These people probably do not have conventionally diversified portfolios – but they really know the markets.

There are bargains in all our investment markets at all times and you will want to take advantage of them. Although you do not want to lose capital neither do you want to be mesmerised by risk. The result then is that you do nothing (or very little) and as an investor, sink somewhere into or below mediocrity.

Instead of trying to avoid risk altogether (which you won't achieve anyway – all investments carry some risk), you should try to manage the risk – and knowledge is probably the best way to do so.

Investment is not a game of chance. You do not need to feel as if your financial affairs are like a leaf in the wind (close your eyes, put your money in and hope – what else can you do?). You can (and should) take control. Empower yourself with knowledge and skill. Acknowledge that all investment carries at least some risk and decide to manage that risk to the best of your ability.

▼SPECIAL NOTE: THE MAD INVENTOR

When I worked as a business consultant I would get at least two calls a month from someone or other who had invented something 'new' which was going to be so popular it would make billions. All the inventor needed was some start-up capital – perhaps $50,000? Did I know someone?

In fact none of these investors was really mad – they were mostly charming, nice people. However, they all had one thing in common – they were incredibly precious (to the point of obsession) about their invention and would hear no criticism either of its engineering, its usefulness or its marketability.

In spite of the fact that every one of these inventions was the greatest thing since the wheel, I don't think a single project was ever successfully brought to the market. As far as I know each one of these inventors still has a mortgage on the house and a garage full of unassembled parts.

There is a lesson here – very few people at the cutting edge of technology make money. Unfair though it is, the people who make money out of technology are those who come along afterwards, once the technology has been proven in the marketplace.

There is the odd exception. However, most investors should stay in the mainstream and keep away from companies floated to develop a new engine or to conduct genetic research to find new medicines. Such investments seldom come off in spite of their huge promise. These investment 'king hits', where you are able to get in on the ground floor of something which truly delivers, are so rare that they should be ignored. Things like newspaper publishers, whiteware manufacturers, retailers and manufacturing companies may sound a bit boring, but as an investment they have a far greater chance of succeeding.

There are two major types of risk. The first is the kind most people think of: loss of capital and poor performance. Loss of capital is easy to understand. The risk of poor performance, however, must be seen in terms of loss of time and therefore loss of opportunity. What else could you have been investing in and profiting from while your investment languishes? The second type of risk is the one that professional fund managers talk about, volatility.

Of the two, the risk of poor investment performance is by far the greater and more important.

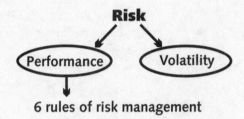

RISK TO PERFORMANCE

Risk to the performance of your investments comes from many sources. There is risk from the economy as a whole, risk from the sector and risk from the individual investments that you have bought. The risk comes from politics (not just in Wellington but in Washington, Canberra and London, since we are rapidly approaching the state of having a global economy), risk from wars, computer bugs, executive fraud and other things seemingly beyond your control (and maybe beyond your knowledge). It's enough to make you start putting bank notes under the mattress (but then what about fire?).

However, all risk can be controlled and managed, dramatically increasing the chances of good performance and decreasing the chances of loss of capital. Note, however, that we can only ever talk about increasing or decreasing the chance of problems – we can never eliminate the possibility. In talking about chances we are talking about statistics and probabilities, not absolutes. If you are going to invest, you are going to take risks – all that needs to be decided is how great those risks will be.

Many of the principles contained in this book are designed to reduce risk while maintaining good returns. The risk-and-return equation (the greater the risk the greater the expected return, and vice versa) has been long recognised. However, considered and principled investment done to a plan will by its very nature considerably reduce risk.

▼ SPECIAL NOTE: INTEREST RATES AND PROPERTY

When interest rates rise, property is hit three times. First, it becomes relatively less attractive as an investment. Investors will, if they can, take their money out of property and put it into bills or bonds. This may take some time to do (property is not a very liquid investment) but there will gradually be less money allocated to property, causing prices to fall.

The second problem with higher interest rates is that some tenants (especially those in commercial and industrial property) will find it harder to pay their rent. A business tenant will find that their interest costs have risen and will therefore try to reduce any other costs that they can, including rent. At the very best, in a high-interest environment tenants will become resistant to rent increases.

The third hit involves property investors' own interest costs. Most property owners have borrowings. The interest on these borrowings usually represents a property investor's greatest expense by far. An increase will either reduce the investment's profitability or, more worrisome, increase the cash deficit. Neither is very attractive.

Property investors should follow a few basic rules for their borrowings:

▼ **Always borrow on a fixed rate.** Your income is fixed, therefore match that with a fixed-interest expense.

▼ **Use any spare income to repay debt.**

▼ **Shop around for the cheapest interest rate.** Even a small reduction in rate can make a very big difference to the total interest that you will pay over the years.

> ▼ **Negotiate hard with your lender for the best deal.**
> ▼ **Always keep a little cash on standby.** If you hit cashflow problems (loss of tenant, hike in interest rates), that cash will become very useful.

Much of risk management is about protecting the downside while advancing the upside. That means having investments that fall less than others when times are bad.

> **Much of risk management is about protecting the downside while advancing the upside.**

In good times (bull runs) in just about any market, the rises are across the board – just about everything goes up. However, bear markets are more erratic – the falls are not uniform nor evenly spread. Some investments are much more recession-proof than others. They may grow a little more slowly (only a little) but will hold their value against the average much better.

The downside is far more damaging to your overall position than the upside is beneficial.

There are six rules that will reduce risk:

1. Buy quality investments
2. If in doubt, stay out
3. It is as easy to sell as it is to buy
4. Diversify
5. Discipline
6. Hedging

1. **Buy quality investments** (see Secret 6). Good quality investments (those with sustainable income) withstand the bad times and recover quicker than those which are more dubious. Make a conscious decision now always to stay with quality.

▼ SPECIAL NOTE: TAKE A WALK

The greatest risk to any investment is a cessation of income. In property investment that usually comes from the loss of a tenant.

Assessing the likely continuance of rental from the sitting tenant is both one of the most important and most difficult tasks for property investors when considering a purchase. This is particularly important for commercial and industrial property where tenants are not so plentiful. With residential property you will generally find a tenant fairly quickly provided that you are willing to meet the market. In commercial and industrial property there are times when there are simply no tenants around, at any price. Ensuring that you have a good long-term tenant at the time of purchase is therefore critical.

You can (and should) do all of the usual things: scrutinise the lease to make sure it is binding, do a credit check on the tenant, ask to look at the present owner's bank statements to make sure the rent is up to date and do a search on the tenant's company if he has one. All of these things will give a pointer to the stability of the tenant.

One other action is to take a quiet walk around the area, without the real estate agent with you. This serves two purposes. The first is that it will give you an idea of how good or bad the area in general is. In particular you should watch for large numbers of 'for lease' signs or vacant properties and for the general busyness of the area. An assessment of that speaks volumes on the strength of the location that you are buying in.

The second effect is that you may get a chance to chat with your possible tenant or the occupiers of neighbouring buildings. Such chats may tell you more than credit checks and company searches.

I was once looking at buying a small industrial property in Christchurch. There was only six months left to go on the lease, and the tenant would not commit himself to renewing it 'at this stage', but the owner's real estate agent assured me that he was bound to renew – after all, he had been there since the building was first built eight years ago.

I took a walk in the area. I wandered into the neighbouring unit and, saying I was looking at buying property in the area, asked what rent the tenant was paying. He told me (grumbling a bit) and then asked what unit I was considering. As soon as he heard it was next door he grinned and asked me if I had a new tenant lined up. The tenant of the building I was interested in had just landed a big long-term contract and his business had doubled. He had been in to his neighbour to see if he could take over his neighbour's premises just a week ago. There was no way he would be renewing the lease in six months.

I didn't buy the property. Tenants would probably be easy enough to find in this area but I did not want the hassle (especially as the property was not going to be discounted). A short walk and a bit of a gossip saved a lot of problems!

2. **If in doubt, stay out.** In assessing investments there will always be good features and bad features. Markets are balanced and uncertain. In any market there are both buyers and sellers, optimists and pessimists. Both of them cannot be right. If you are not sure, sit tight and wait. There will be other good investments; there always are.

3. **It is as easy to sell as it is to buy.** This particularly applies to shares and bonds; property can be considerably more difficult. The real point here is that if you make a mistake by buying the wrong investment, cut your losses. Do not fall into the trap that many investors do when they are showing losses which sees them refusing to sell until they get their money back.

If you make a mistake by buying the wrong investment, cut your losses.

You should always look to the future – the past is only useful in that you can learn from your mistakes. If you are uneasy about an investment, ask yourself the following question: If I did not own this investment and the opportunity arose to buy it, would I take up the opportunity to buy? If the answer to that is 'no', then you should sell. Being a holder of an investment is to be a bull and is the same effective position as being a buyer.

4. **Diversify.** Everyone needs a diversified investment portfolio to some extent – but not one that is overdone. It is possible to diversify to such a degree that you can only achieve average returns at best.

   Diversification is summed up by the 'don't put all of your eggs in one basket' adage. It can be invaluable, especially for conservative investors and those looking for long-term savings. Fund managers who control balanced funds hold portfolios with a little property, some equities, some bonds, a little cash and some offshore investments. Each investment type will perform well at different times and under different economic conditions, meaning that the funds will tend to show steady (but never spectacular) returns over long periods of time. This type of fund usually returns around 6-8% pa – perhaps 4-5% over the rate of inflation, which is a fairly reasonable return for someone who is investing conservatively for decades (maybe for superannuation purposes) although there are many people who will want to do better.

▼ SPECIAL NOTE: OFFSHORE INVESTMENT

The greatest form of diversification is to invest offshore. Many New Zealanders do this through international equities trusts or international bonds trusts and a few people invest offshore directly into equities or property. By investing offshore you are getting away from New Zealand's very small and narrow investment markets and decreasing your exposure to the New Zealand economy. Offshore investment has five main advantages:

▼ New Zealand investment markets do not rate in an international sense – they are tiny.

▼ Many overseas countries have performed far better economically than New Zealand over the last few decades.

▼ You are increasing your diversification – more baskets for your eggs.

▼ You can access industries (especially in high technology) which are not available for investment in New Zealand.

▼ There is a natural currency hedge if you travel overseas a lot. By having assets in a country to which you travel frequently, you are protected to some degree at least from a fall in the New Zealand dollar. Such a fall could make it very expensive to travel to that country. However, if you have assets there, the Kiwi dollar falling will mean that these investments will have risen in value in New Zealand dollar terms.

However, there are some disadvantages:

▼ You will have a currency risk. The investment gains that you make overseas can be wiped out by a strengthening in the New Zealand dollar.

▼ It is hard to manage and monitor your investments from New Zealand since it is difficult to find information and keep track of what is happening. (A computer online helps this considerably.)

▼ The legal, financial and business systems are different overseas.

These three disadvantages are particularly great if you are wanting to invest directly overseas. Indeed, there are very few of us with the skill or time to invest directly offshore. My experience with people who have done this has not been good. People owning property in Australia (which is closest to New Zealand both geographically and in terms of our legal and business environment) have often struck difficulty. Australia can seem a long way away when you are having trouble finding a new tenant for your investment property. There are investors who have been sold Gold Coast apartments and have regretted their purchases almost immediately.

Australia can seem a long way away when you are having trouble finding a new tenant.

The costs and difficulties of direct offshore property investment are such that a higher return is necessary for you to be bothered. The currency risk should be managed by borrowing as much as possible in the currency of the country that the property is in. Send as little New Zealand currency as possible – only the funds that you remit are exposed to currency risk. Have your property managed and be sure that you have the full range of dependable professional advisers (investment adviser, accountant, lawyer, mortgage broker, real estate agent) – you will almost certainly need them at some time.

Most people should invest overseas with a fund manager.

Most people should invest overseas with a fund manager. Good fund managers have branches or agencies in all of the world's main financial centres who will be well informed on local market conditions. The fund manager will manage the currency risk (as far as possible) and although your potential returns may not be quite as good, it will save you some sleepless nights.

I think, however, that diversification can be overdone.

The most successful investors are those who analyse carefully and then take a strong position. They are people who back themselves to make the right decision and because they work from a plan with definite rules and principles are far more often right than wrong.

Some of the people who invest like this will still have a diversified portfolio. They may have a range of good investments giving them a strong overall financial position. They may have a mortgage-free house and a good superannuation fund, but use any spare money to invest in just two or three shares or into one property.

The key to this strategy is that they analyse and consider carefully before acting. They are prepared to put their eggs into one basket – but they make very sure that it is a good basket and that they are on a firm footing.

Diversification will inevitably cut risk and return. You need to establish where you fit in the overall equation – how aggressive do you want to be given your skill levels and financial position?

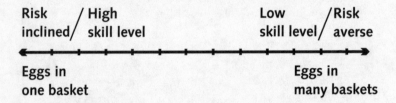

Diversification Continuum

Where do <u>you</u> fit?

Risk inclined / High skill level		Low skill level / Risk averse
Eggs in one basket		Eggs in many baskets

There may also be lifestyle considerations. I once knew someone with less than $100,000 in the sharemarket spread across 40 companies in New Zealand, Australia, UK and Singapore. This would have driven most people mad – 40 annual and interim reports to read, 80 (fairly small) dividend cheques to bank, files to keep track of each investment, etc. But this gentleman (who was retired) loved it! It was his interest and hobby. Financially he had diversified himself to the point where his portfolio was always going to perform much the same as the indices – his was a very defensive position. And yet he had an interesting hobby – and that was what he wanted.

5. **Discipline.** The best investors are disciplined individuals. They set financial parameters and yardsticks, and stick to them. They have a plan and, ignoring much of the heat and noise of the market, they stick to that plan.

> The best investors are disciplined individuals.

For example, an investor might own some Telecom shares which are trading at a dividend yield of 5% –

a return she regards as reasonable for that company. She might then decide that if the share price went up so that the dividend yield was 3.5% she would sell (because at that level they are overpriced) but if the shares ever fell so that the dividend yield was 6.5% she would buy some more (because at that level they are cheap).

This investor would stick to that plan (unless something major happened), ignoring the hype of the market. She has made a calm, rational decision and set parameters which she follows scrupulously.

This sort of discipline is never as easy as it sounds! If Telecom shares have fallen to be on a dividend yield of 6.5%, there is likely to be a fair bit of doom and gloom around the markets and in the media. It is not easy to stand against that sort of tide and buy anyway.

▼ SPECIAL NOTE: WHEN THINGS GO WRONG

Things do go wrong in investment. With geared investments (see **Secret 7**) especially, things going wrong can be serious and require prompt corrective action.

▼ Review the investment. If it is unlikely to recover soon (ie, you made a mistake) get out of it if you can, taking a loss if necessary. This may not be easy to do (particularly if it is a property investment) but if you can, put your money, time and energy into something which will work. Rapid action is essential once you realise that you have made a mistake.

▼ Talk to your lender. When things go wrong with geared investments you are not the only one with a problem – your lender has one too. Co-operation is nearly always the best way to come to an arrangement – that requires honest dialogue between you and your lender.

Beware the ostrich

Procrastination, denial and the blaming of others is the worst approach.

syndrome – there is no point in hiding your head in the sand and hoping that the problem will go away – it won't. An honest unbiased appraisal of the situation followed by firm, fast and decisive action is the best cure. Procrastination, denial and the blaming of others is the worst approach.

6. **Hedging.** It is possible with some investments (equities and bonds in particular) to use futures or options markets to cover the downside. This is a difficult area requiring expert advice but is not beyond some private investors; the use of 'derivatives' can be a real option in times of uncertainty.

Derivatives are so called because they derive from some real or underlying asset, such as bonds or equities. They can be used as a type of insurance cover if you are faced with an uncertain or difficult market.

Imagine that you hold a portfolio of shares. Economic chaos in Asia has you worried about the state of the share-market. You could sell all your shares but this might take some time and be quite expensive. Instead of doing that you call a broker and 'sell the index' (the index is really an artificial share portfolio which if you have a spread of shares will perform much the same as your own real or physical portfolio).

When you have 'sold short' while you still hold your share portfolio one of two things may happen:

▼ The market falls. If this happens you will have a loss on your real portfolio but you will make a profit on the futures transaction, meaning that you stay in the same position.

▼ The market rises, in which case you will make a loss on the futures transaction but the value of your share portfolio will have risen to compensate.

Either way you are in the same position. Many institutional investors use derivatives to cover their investments and protect their downside. Some 'investors' trade and speculate in such things, while others use them only as insurance. It is even possible to use them to develop a synthetic portfolio, ie, to buy the index rather than buy a portfolio of real shares.

Derivative markets work because you can sell an asset before you own it. Selling 'short' (it is called 'short' because you are short of the asset that you are selling – you don't actually have it) has the effect of allowing you to make a profit in a falling market. You sell the asset at a certain level, buying it back in later at a lower price to square off your position (assuming that you were right and the market did indeed fall). The profit on this transaction occurs because you have sold for more than what you will buy at in the future.

> **Selling 'short' has the effect of allowing you to make a profit in a falling market.**

The world of derivatives is an arcane one and there are details (and difficulties) far beyond the simple explanation given above. It is something that you would need to be very well advised on before becoming involved. Nevertheless, futures contracts and options can provide a relatively quick form of insurance for investors and should not be overlooked entirely because of their unfamiliarity.

> **Derivative markets work because you can sell an asset before you own it.**

▼ SPECIAL NOTE: GUARANTEED RETURN

You often see new apartments being offered as investments with a guaranteed rental return for a period. The advertisement screams out its promise – *Guaranteed 9% pa for 2 years.*

I am always a bit cynical. Why, I ask, if this is such a well located and beautifully fitted-out apartment does the developer need to give a performance guarantee? What happens in two year's time? And, most important of all, who is really paying for any rental shortfall?

Why is a guarantee needed? The official answer to that is that it might take a little time to get the occupancy rates up to budget, to a level which will pay the costs of the apartment and support it as an investment. So that you, the investor, can get a return immediately (and therefore in most cases cover your borrowings) the developer (in his generosity) will make sure that you are getting a reasonable yield from day one.

The real reason is of course that it makes the apartments easier to sell. Investors are most likely to borrow to purchase their units but banks will be reluctant to lend if there is insufficient rental return to pay the interest. By making it easy for investors to find finance, the developer sells more apartments.

In fact, experience shows that apartments which are good, that meet the market well, satisfying what is required, do not need a guarantee. Those which are well located, well appointed and well timed are snapped up.

What happens in two year's time? The projections usually show that by that time, occupancy rates will have risen so that the investment is standing on its own feet (if not positively booming). A more cynical view would be that the developer has sold the apartment, paid the guaranteed rental and is gone. Whether reality matches the projections is no longer his concern – it is yours.

Who really pays the guaranteed rental? Officially, of course, the developer does. In reality, you do! The amount of the guarantee payment has already been loaded into the price. If you did not get the guarantee, you should be able to buy the apartment cheaper. When the developer has done his costings, the likely amount of any guarantee payment will have been budgeted for (it has probably come out of his marketing budget). It is unlikely that the developer will cut his profit margin – he simply loads up the price a little.

I would not necessarily reject out of hand any investment that heavily promotes a rental guarantee. But I am cynical and experienced enough to know that property developers do not offer these out of the goodness of their hearts (assuming that you could ever find a developer with a heart). They give them because they sell more apartments quicker and at better prices.

First and foremost, any investment must stand (and run) on its own feet, with or without a guarantee.

VOLATILITY

Risk volatility is the amount by which investments fluctuate above and below their expected returns. It really has little to do with the ultimate performance of an investment, or little to do with where it ends up – instead it is about the thrashing around that it does while it gets there.

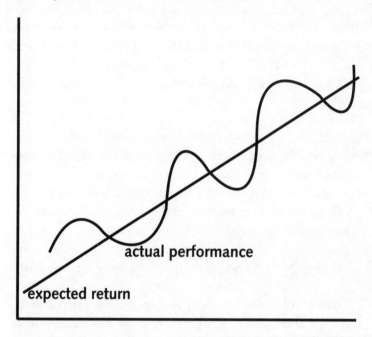

The amount that the investment goes above or below the expected return line is the investment's volatility. It is measured by what statisticians call 'standard deviation'.

Volatility is not very important for most long-term private investors. Provided you have decided to invest for some years (or even decades) and you are confident that your investment is a good one and will eventually perform, you will only be concerned with the investment getting to where you want it and not with how it actually gets there. You may, however, need good nerves holding a volatile investment as it may fall alarmingly, only to rise again. The temptation to sell (possibly at a loss) during these fluctuations is great.

BETA

Beta is a measurement of the amount that a particular asset deviates from the overall market. Again, it is not a measure of performance (and is therefore of less interest to private investors) but of the movements of a particular investment relative to others.

For example, a particular share may rise much more steeply than the total sharemarket rises but fall much more when the market falls. Beta measures the relativity between the share and the sharemarket overall. A share which has a Beta of 1 will vary to the same degree as the market. One with a Beta of 2 will vary twice as much as the market and one with a Beta of 0.5 will vary half as much.

There are three groups who are concerned with volatility:

▼ **Traders.** These are people who are not in the market for the long term but who want to buy low and sell high over short periods (days and weeks). These people actually like highly volatile assets as the swings that they try to pick and take advantage of are bigger.

▼ **Short-term investors.** These are people who have a use for the invested money in, say, a few months. They hate volatility. It is not a good idea to put such short-term money in a volatile investment because at the very time you need the money the investment may be on one of its periodic down ticks. I have always thought that bank deposits (or similar) are the best place for short-term money.

Bank deposits are the best place for short-term money.

▼ **Institutional investors.** Fund managers need to be concerned with volatility because they want to give good, consistent returns. Each month or quarter or year, they advertise their returns and want them to be consistently good. This is not to say that fund managers steer away completely from volatile investments – they don't. Telecom is a moderately volatile investment but institutions have invested heavily in that.

Instead the fund managers diversify to take the volatility out of their portfolio. Modern Portfolio Theory (a theory of diversifying assets in a portfolio) requires that fund managers use computer modelling to determine which investment should be purchased to reduce volatility. This is a very sophisticated process involving complicated statistical method.

There is perhaps one reason why private investors should keep an eye on an investment's volatility. A sudden movement in the investment price may be a tell-tale sign of something happening – either good or bad.

For example, you own a share valued at around 400¢. Usually it moves in 3-5¢ jumps between a range of 380¢ and 420¢. But suddenly it rises to 470¢ in jumps of 20¢. This is almost certainly a sign that something is going on – perhaps an announcement is due and the smart money is pouring in. It is an indicator that you need to get active to find out what is happening.

It works just as well on the downside. A fall to say 330¢ is probably a sign that something adverse has happened. You need to find out what it is!

There have been many attempts to measure risk and volatility and whole books written on the subject. While much of this measurement and the theories which arise from it may be very interesting you must always remember that these measurements are based on past performance. You of course are investing for the future. While past performance is a reasonable indicator of what will happen in the future, it is no guarantee. Nor is an overall measurement of the risk of an investment – at best it can only tell you what is likely to happen. For example, in New Zealand, corporate bonds would be measured as fairly low risk. That will be of little comfort to those who invested in Skellerup bonds and lost money!

▼ SPECIAL NOTE: 100% PROPERTY

One of the seemingly risky investment strategies that many Kiwis have followed is to put all their eggs in the property basket. There are many New Zealanders who have purchased a rental property as their own little retirement investment and have all their wealth tied up in houses. I have written about this in two other books, concluding that it is perhaps less risky than it sounds, provided that they are not speculating in low yield houses. This is because such people adopted hands-on management styles, they look after their properties and manage them tightly. It is also because most property in New Zealand has performed very well as an investment and most property investors recognise that they must invest for long periods of time.

However, financial experts would say that investment property is a fairly volatile asset – and probably it is. Property values do go up and down quite a lot.

In spite of this, one of the beauties of property investment is its apparent lack of volatility. This is because you are unlikely to have property valued very often and are therefore unaware of changes in value. Ignorance is bliss!

Paradoxically, that ignorance leads to good investment behaviour. Many equity and bond traders react emotionally and instinctively because they see the value of their investments in the newspaper over breakfast each morning. They buy or sell on the basis of what they see (frequently reading half-baked media commentary) and without stopping to consider.

Property investors who have purchased wisely (thinking first and foremost about their cash yield), continue to bank the rent in spite of what may or may not be happening, oblivious to any short-term ups or down, carrying on regardless. What's volatility?

Buy Quality

▼ ▼ ▼ ▼

*'No investor has ever
regretted buying
quality investments.'*

NO INVESTOR HAS EVER REGRETTED BUYING quality investments. Large numbers have, however, regretted chasing high returns by going into lesser investments. Quality investments do better on the upside than most investments and withstand the downturns better. Put together, these two attributes are quite remarkable – performance with safety.

> **Speculative binges characteristically involve people buying 'investments' with no income.**

In investment terms, quality is easy to define: a quality investment is one with good sustainable income which is likely to grow. This means different things in each of the three investment classes (see page 52) but in all cases it is the nature of the income which is important.

It is always interesting how, after a boom followed by a bust, there is a call for a retreat to quality. This is usually after the excesses of a boom have meant an abandonment of quality and, in a spectacular frenzy, an abandonment of the principles of investment – the secrets of investment are lost, temporarily at least. Speculative binges characteristically involve people buying 'investments' with no income – the profits (bound to be huge!) are promised for some time in the future. The boom is caused principally by there being not enough quality investments to satisfy the demand from investors. A principled, thinking investor will recognise that she is better to stay with quality and if in a boom she cannot find quality investments, she should stay out.

Some might say that you can do better with more speculative investments. For example you could perhaps buy some 'penny dreadful' shares at 3¢. If they go to 4¢ you have made 33%, probably very quickly. Provided that you get out, you have done very well. Similarly you could buy an old rundown house in a good area. You do some quick cosmetic work on it (paint it, and manicure the garden) and you may be able to sell it on quickly for thousands more than it owes you.

However, these are trading or speculative activities, not investment. They may produce spectacular profits; but then again they may turn into nothing. The only thing that they have in common with investment is that they happen to operate in the same markets and with the same assets. The difference is similar to the one between an author and a book retailer – they both work with books but perform very different tasks and use very different skills.

> **If you are an investor, stay with quality.**

If you are going to trade or speculate, you may at times want to be in low-quality assets. Cheap shares and property are often very volatile and show large percentage swings. However, if you are an investor, stay with quality.

There are good reasons why quality investments outperform ordinary ones – reasons explained by arithmetic. Investments are valued by their income (see **Secret 3**), by applying a 'multiplier' to their annual income. This multiplier as a factor may be expressed as a P:E ratio or a capitalisation rate or a yield. Whatever it is called, annual income (profits from shares/businesses, rental from property, interest from deposits) is multiplied by a factor.

The most straightforward way to approach this is by looking at shares and the price: earnings ratio. The P:E ratio is the number of times the earnings of a company goes into its share price. So the P:E ratio is about valuing a share by its annual earnings. A very good company's share might be valued at 16 times its annual earnings, an average company's shares at 10 times annual earnings and a poor company's shares at perhaps 6 times annual earnings. Because of this valuation method, the share price will rise as annual earnings rise. If the earnings go up, the P:E ratio will be applied to those higher earnings. Every dollar of additional earning is multiplied by the earnings ratio to get a new, higher valuation. If that very good company can increase its profit by $1000, its worth will rise by $16,000.

The really interesting thing is that the better companies, the ones with higher P:E ratios, will have their increased earnings multiplied by a higher (or greater) number and so they will show a greater increase in share price. Provided that their prospects all remain the same and the market continues to rate them with similar P:E ratios, the companies with higher P:E ratios will have better share price growth than lower-rated companies even though earnings have increased by the same amount.

Imagine three companies each of different quality (and therefore with different P:E ratios) but all of which happen to have the same share price. Here are the valuations:

	e.p.s	P:E Ratio	Share Price
Company A (poor)	30 cps	6	180¢
Company B (average)	18 cps	10	180¢
Company C (good)	11.25 cps	16	180¢

Now let's look at what happens if all companies managed to increase their earnings by 2 cents per share:

	eps	P:E Ratio	Share Price	Increased eps	P:E Ratio	New Share Price	Gain
Company A (poor)	30 cps	6	180¢	32 cps	6	192¢	+6%
Company B (average)	18 cps	10	180¢	20 cps	10	200¢	+11%
Company C (good)	11.25 cps	16	180¢	13.25 cps	16	212¢	+18%

The better quality, higher rated share (Company C) has gained 18% against 11% and 6% gain for the other two. This is simply because the additional 2cps of earnings is multiplied by a higher factor (the P:E ratio).

These figures are of course unlikely to work out as neatly as this in practice. For a start, the prospects of the companies and the market overall would need to remain the same. Second, earnings are not likely to increase in the manner above. In fact it is most likely that the quality share will increase its earnings faster than the other two both in percentage and absolute terms, giving even greater gains. That in turn may lead to the sharemarket rating the share on a higher P:E ratio, pushing up the price even further.

Nevertheless in principle it is right in that every additional cent of earnings is multiplied by a bigger factor with a corresponding greater shift in share price. It's also right in practice as anyone who has watched markets and invested for long periods will tell you – quality shares do better.

This works just as well for property investment. While property is valued by its yield (or capitalisation rate), in effect the annual rent is multiplied by the reciprocal of the yield. Thus a building which has a 9% yield is valued by multiplying the rent by 11.11 (which is the inverse of 9). You can divide the rent by its yield to get the value or multiply by the inverse – it is the same thing.

For example, take a building with an annual net rental of $10,000 pa. Depending upon its quality (good, average or poor) it would be valued like this:

good property $10,000 rent 9% yield = $111,111 (reciprocal 11.11)
average property $10,000 rent 10% yield = $100,000 (reciprocal 10)
poor property $10,000 rent 11% yield = $90,909 (reciprocal 9.09)

The reciprocal (or multiplier) for the good property is greater than for the poor quality property. Therefore every dollar of extra rent will be multiplied by a greater factor.

Let's imagine that at rent review time, all three owners negotiated a rent rise of $50 per week, taking the rent from $10,000 pa to $12,500 pa.

	Good	Average	Poor
Current Rent	$10,000 pa	$10,000 pa	$10,000 pa
Appropriate Yield	9%	10%	11%
Reciprocal/Multiplier	11.11	10	9.09
Current Value	$111,000	$100,000	$90,909
New Rent	$12,500	$12,500	$12,500
Value	$138,889	$125,000	$113,636
Increase in Value	$27,777	$25,000	$22,727

That extra $50 per week of rent is multiplied by different factors and of course the quality property does better – following the rent rise there is $27,777 of capital gain but only $22,727 for the poor property. The effect of gearing can magnify this gain greatly.

Like the share example, the figures will of course not work out in practice as neatly as this. In fact, just like the share example, the good property is likely to enjoy even better capital growth than the others because rentals rise further and faster with better property. Nevertheless, in spite of the fact that the figures may not work out as neatly as this, any experienced investor will tell you that this does hold true in the real world – quality investments perform better.

SAFETY

Not only do better quality investments give better returns, they are safer. This may seem at variance with that old adage about the higher the risk the higher return, nevertheless for principled investors who are prepared to be patient, it is true.

The reason that better quality investments are safer is simply because of their income. By definition, good investments have good income. This income keeps flowing in good times and in bad – even though times might be bad and the capital value of your investment founders and even falls in the short or medium term, you can take comfort from the fact that you are still getting a good cash return.

There is a huge amount of safety in continuing cashflow.

There is a huge amount of safety in continuing cashflow. Not only can you use or enjoy that cashflow but it makes the sale of the investment possible at a reasonable level (if that proves to be necessary). The investments which have real problems are those where the cash stops flowing or those which have been purchased on the basis of high income at some time in the distant future, (which high income never eventuates). The investments which do not have trouble (or at least less trouble and for shorter time) are those where the income is secure.

Provided the profits/rents/interest are sustained you will always be able to sell your investment. You may have to negotiate the price a bit and in bad times give a discount but there will be a market for what you own. You should compare that with some investments which you may not be able to sell at almost any price. An empty building can sit unsold for years (a building I know which cost $7.5 million sat empty for three years before finally being sold at under $1.7 million). Shares can collapse in value, sometimes within days when profits fall. Regardless of the market, quality investments can be sold fairly quickly with, at worst, a small discount.

So, given that quality investments are about security of income, how does this then relate to the three different investment types, and how do you spot quality?

INTEREST-EARNING DEPOSITS

While most people think of deposits as either putting your money in the bank or buying bonds, there are in fact many types of interest-earning deposits. You can give your money to anything or anyone you like to get interest. The only real quality issue is that the borrower meets the agreed interest and returns the capital on due date. Given this, there are two things that you need to consider: the borrower itself and any security provided.

THE BORROWER

This may be anyone from the New Zealand Government to your nephew borrowing $5,000 from you to buy a car, with every imaginable category in between. Obviously, the better the standing of the borrower, the lower the interest rate they are likely to pay.

The most common type of institution that people lend money to is of course a bank. Most people would consider one of the mainstream banks as a fairly good risk. This cannot, however, be taken for granted. In the last decade or so the Bank of New Zealand went very close to failing and needed substantial cash injections from its shareholders.

Because of this, you would think that you should check out the creditworthiness of any borrower before you lend to them. If that was necessary, we would see tens of thousands of members of the public trying to do a credit check before allowing their salaries to be paid into their bank account – clearly not practicable, even if people had the necessary skills to run the credit checks.

Instead, most major borrowing institutions (governments, local authorities, banks and major corporates) have their standing and worthiness rated by a credit-rating agency (Standard & Poor's or Moodys are the best known). These organisations are completely independent and after analysing and scrutinising the books and accounts of the borrower give it a score, perhaps AA+ or B – . (Just to confuse things a little, both Moodys and Standard & Poor's use slightly different scoring systems.) These credit ratings are sufficiently well done and independent so that we can rely on them. If there is a change in the borrower's circumstances the agencies are likely to put the borrower on 'credit watch' pending another lot of scrutinising and analysing.

The rating that a borrower gets is important as it dictates what interest rate it will pay for its borrowings. You often see in the news media that the New Zealand Government has had its rating affirmed or had it raised or lowered. This is not simply of academic interest or something for politicians to fight over – large institutional investors in particular (the so-called gnomes of Zurich) use that rating to decide whether they will or will not lend, and at what interest rate. Given that the New Zealand Government has borrowed tens of billions of dollars, even a reduction of 0.05% is a substantial amount of interest. Major corporates (whether state or privately owned) may also be rated and publish that rating at times when they are raising capital. Again, if they have a good rating they will find money easier and cheaper to borrow.

Most banks are also rated by an agency. This is a matter of public record. In spite of the problems which Bank of New Zealand had in the past, at the time of writing all of New Zealand's major banks (including Bank of New Zealand) have good solid credit ratings meaning that you can relax when your salary is direct credited to your bank account.

Finance companies also take deposits from investors. Such companies can vary in size from quite large institutions which are subsidiaries of banks (eg, UDC, AGC and BNZ Finance) to very small companies, just once removed from loan sharks. Few of these will have the creditworthiness of banks and therefore will pay a higher interest rate. Even the quite large finance companies which are subsidiaries of banks will not usually be as financially strong as their parents. Nor do their parent banks necessarily guarantee their smaller offspring – in the event of a crisis in one of these finance companies, the bank which owns it would be under no obligation to bail it or the depositers out (and in reality may refuse to do so).

Smaller, second- or third-tier finance companies will vary hugely in their creditworthiness. Personally, I would not invest in one of these unless there was good security available.

There are a few other opportunities to make interest-bearing deposits. Some people lend friends and family money although that is fraught with difficulty. Solicitors' mortgage nominee companies are now much less common than they were, as are contributory mortgage companies (especially with the demise of RSL). One area which is worth considering for many short-term investors is that of the cash management unit trusts which are offered by some of the fund managers. Although what is offered is not a direct interest-bearing deposit (you are purchasing units in a trust), these funds usually invest in wholesale money markets, bank bills, bonds, mortgages, etc, and often pay a net interest rate above that which you would get at the bank. The fact that you can access them conveniently by telephone makes them well worth considering.

SECURITY

When a bank or finance company lends you money, they almost always require security, a mortgage over your house or chattel security over your car on hire purchase. Similarly, when you make a deposit with some organisations you may be offered security. In the case of very good borrowers (governments, local body authorities, strong corporates, and banks) there is no security. Their word (and their credit rating) is enough for most investors – they will invest without security. By lending money to one of these organisations you become an unsecured creditor and rank behind nearly everyone else to get paid in the event of difficulties.

However, smaller corporates and finance companies will often give security to lenders, usually in the form of a debenture – without security no one will lend them money or invest (or at least will require a very high interest rate to do so). A debenture is like a mortgage – it gives the lender who holds it a charge over the company's assets (debtors, stock, plant and equipment, etc) so that the debenture holder gets paid before creditors and lenders who do not have the same security. Security relates mostly to priority and ranking. In the event of a company becoming insolvent, creditors and lenders are not all lumped together and paid the same amount. Instead, some are paid out before others – those who hold security over assets are paid before those who are unsecured. If there is nothing left after the secured creditors have been paid, then the unsecured lenders will get nothing. This ranking is well established in law and any creditor or lender can easily find out where she ranks in the event of receivership or liquidation.

Sometimes, finance companies and small corporates will have more than one secured creditor and these will be ranked in turn. For example you will often see finance companies in advertisements offering second- (or third-) ranking debenture stock. The interest rate offered will be greater than the first debenture holders get, which reflects the poorer security and greater risk. Smaller corporates who issue bonds also usually offer a lower ranking to the bondholders than they do to their bankers. For example, Skellerup bondholders ranked in security after the banks (although

Corporates and finance companies do fail.

the bondholders did rank above the company's unsecured trade creditors).

If you as an investor are going to move away from quality deposits you really do need security. Corporates and finance companies do fail; consider carefully before chasing higher returns. There are many people who have had difficulties and who would say (with the benefit of experience) that bank deposits have much to commend them.

PROPERTY

Quality in property investment is made up of three things:

TENANT AND LEASE

This is most important for commercial and industrial property where leases are longer (frequently 6 years and more) and tenants can be hard to come by. When commercial or industrial property becomes empty it can be months and occasionally years before you get a new tenant. If sustainability of income is important, a good tenant bound by a long-term lease is critical. Not only is a tenant of good standing less likely to breach its obligations, but a good tenant is able to pay any increased rent that you can assess at rent review time – I have often seen tenants at rent review agree that the landlord's suggested rent is fair but then plead poverty, saying that their business simply cannot afford to pay it. (My response to that particular tactic is to ask the tenant to prove their claims of poverty by providing a statement of position and relevant financial information.)

Quite clearly you are likely to pay more (and accept a lower yield) for a building which is leased to IBM for 12 years than a building leased to a local panelbeater for 18 months. As an investor, if you are risk-averse and security-conscious, you are better to concentrate on the tenant and lease to make sure that they are strong since they are your first consideration in security of cashflow. Risk-averse property investors who lack the capital to go into the top end of the market should consider accessing property via a unit trust or syndicate, rather than compromise themselves too much.

> **A good tenant bound by a long-term lease is critical.**

LOCATION

A good location is one that is in demand by tenants – people want to rent there. This of course means different things for different types of property: for residential property it will be a building close to town or shops, on a bus route, handy to schools, etc, while for an industrial building (a warehouse or factory) it will be on a main arterial route with easy access to the port or airport. A good location will be where a building is surrounded by buildings which are of a similar type and use and which are in demand from tenants. That demand will drive up rentals which will in turn fuel the growth in value of the property.

Concentration on a good location is for investors who are looking for growth more than security, although a good location does help with security because if your building becomes empty it

> **A good location is one that is in demand by tenants.**

is easier to find tenants. This is not as important as having a good tenant and lease in the first place. Because of the likely rental and capital growth you will certainly pay a higher price (accept a lower yield) for flats in Mt Eden or St Albans than you will on the outskirts of Cricklewood.

THE BUILDING ITSELF

This is simply an assessment of the age of the building, its serviceability, attractiveness and likely future maintenance. A new permanent-material building is important for those who are reluctant to spend too much time managing their property investments. This is especially important in residential property. You would surely accept a lower yield and pay a higher price for a brand new, permanent-material building than for an old wooden structure.

These three things make up the quality of your property investments. However you should be aware that it is hard (or impossible) to find the perfect property: a new well-built structure, superbly located and leased long-term to a good tenant. All of these attributes are unlikely to be perfectly in place – you are going to have to compromise.

The way in which you compromise is personal to you and requires thought. If you are an aggressive investor looking for growth you will compromise towards a good location, putting less emphasis on the lease and tenant; if you need security of income look for a good tenant and lease; if you want an easily managed property find something new and made out of permanent materials although if you do have spare time, skill and inclination you may want to buy a rundown building to do up. Property investment can be many things to different people – decide what sort of person and what sort of investor you are.

Property Quality Assessment

Property features	Investor's risk sensitivity	High growth required	Investor's time available
Lease and tenant	very important	important	important
Location	important	very important	less important
Building configuration	less important	less important	very important

For most small private investors it is this necessity to compromise (along with an aversion to property management and the reluctance to borrow large sums) which puts off many people from property investment. They reason that if they cannot buy the best (or at least very good) property, then they should stay out.

An alternative strategy is to have exposure to property investment through some form of managed fund, listed company or syndicate. These groups do have the money required (perhaps tens of millions of dollars), the expertise and management to own the (near) perfect property investment. They really do own well located, near-new buildings leased to IBM for 12 years. By buying into them, you can own at least a part of such a quality investment with no management worries.

A small share in a good property is better than 100% of a white elephant.

This will cost you, of course, but it is better than having no exposure to property at all (or being led to compromise too far on quality). A small share in a good property is better than 100% of a white elephant.

▼SPECIAL NOTE: WHITE ELEPHANTS

Property investors play with very big numbers and there are many traps for the unwary. Mistakes in purchasing property investments can be serious if not fatal (financially).

There are white elephants in property investment, nearly always camouflaged as bargains. They are often offered on very high yields or some other generous terms (perhaps vendor finance). Although there are a lot of genuine bargains available you do need to be very careful. Sign a contract subject to finance and due diligence and then spend some time (and money) checking it out.

Check these things:

▼ **Most buildings carry white elephant status because of their location**. More often than not it is because the building is in an area which is not suitable for its use – a warehouse in a residential area, flats in an industrial area, shops out in the country. Often the building was built for a specific purpose and a specific occupier, both of which have since passed. Once the purpose and use no longer apply the building is essentially valueless. Even if you do find a tenant the building is unlikely to show much growth over the years. Similarly in small towns and rural areas of New Zealand – many of these are declining. Sad though that may be, you should not make your property investments in any place which is not strong, vibrant, growing and diversified.

▼ **Difficult tenants are often a cause of white elephant status**. Even tenants who seem good may in fact be difficult to deal with, exasperating the owner. You do not want to take over someone else's problems.

▼ **Zoning can be a problem for some buildings**. Sometimes a building will be out of its correct zoning but may continue to be used while the existing tenants are there. When those tenants leave you could have problems. This is a relatively easy matter for your solicitor to check out.

▼ **Unusual lease terms can cause difficulties**. Leases to small companies which are not guaranteed, rent reviews every 5 years instead of the more usual 2 years and clauses allowing the tenant to give early notice to quit may not be common but do exist. Again, your solicitor will be able to advise you.

▼ **Design problems can make a building a white elephant**. Things like layout of offices – roller doors that are not high enough, structural posts and pillars which restrict movement, unusually shaped rooms – will all reduce the number of uses of a building and the rent that will be paid.

The best way to deal with white elephants and poorer quality properties generally is not to buy them in the first place. Remember that the 'greater fool' theory no longer applies. This theory, popular in the boom times of the 1970s and 1980s, said that it mattered little if you bought something foolish because before long a greater fool than you would come along and take the problem off your hands (in those days probably at a price sufficient to give you a good profit!). The investment markets are now far more demanding and discerning; there may not be a bigger fool than you willing to take your mistakes and problems off your hands.

If you do make a mistake, in property or in any other investment area for that matter, sell it at the best price you can – taking a loss if necessary. You need to get your money out of your mistake and into something which will work for you. To do that you will need to meet the market. There is no point in hoping that the market will come back to meet you – it probably won't and may get worse rather than better.

SHARES

Like any other desirable investment, quality shares offer good income. However, it is harder to judge the precise nature of that income with shares, partly because many companies are not very forthcoming with information and partly because it may require financial analytic skills to make much use of the information that you do get.

When buying shares, always keep in mind that you are buying a business; not all of a business, perhaps, but a part or a share of a business. If you keep this firmly in your mind, much of the analysis of companies becomes common sense. You know that a company whose business is drilling holes in the ground looking for oil is likely to be more risky than one whose business is retailing clothing; a business which makes and sells bread and pies will have quite different prospects from a trucking firm.

Substantially, all you are doing is deciding what sort of business you want to be a part of and which sort you do not.

▼ SPECIAL NOTE: WHAT DRIVES THE SHAREMARKET?

Although investors in the sharemarket may appear to behave like reef fish at times, there are usually good reasons for what happens – in the longer term at least.

Above all else, the sharemarket needs a climate of certainty to prosper – all markets (but especially the sharemarket) hate uncertainty, a feeling that the rules may change after money has gone in. In a climate of uncertainty investors will follow the adage: 'If in doubt, stay out.'

All markets hate uncertainty.

The sharemarket responds to these factors:

▼ **Political activity.** If the government looks unstable or, worse, some left-wing politician looks like getting the country's chequebook, the market will react very badly. In the lead-up to an election the sharemarket acts as a very accurate barometer, giving a better idea of the probable result than most pollsters. Note that it is often the actual anticipation of an unfriendly government which is worse – once the new government takes over (and the worst has happened) the market often heaves a sigh of relief and gets on with it. It now knows the new rules and finds it can live with them.

▼ **Interest rates.** Investments compete against each other. If interest rates are high, money will go to bonds or bank bills from the sharemarket.

▼ **Business confidence/economic growth.** The sharemarket usually leads the economy itself by 6-12 months –

buoyancy on the market points to a coming economic upturn and vice versa. Businesses that are listed on the sharemarket want to operate in a growing economy, confident that things like inflation, exchange rates and interest rates are stable.

▼ **Liquidity.** The degree to which investors are cashed up pushes the market along. A lot of takeover activity means that shareholders are bought-out; these bought out shareholders have to do something with their cash – inevitably some finds its way back into the market. Takeover activity also tends to push up prices because when a company has been taken over there are fewer shares that investors may purchase. Similarly when companies return capital to shareholders or buy back their own shares, investors put at least some of the proceeds into other companies, driving up prices.

Remember always that the sharemarket is a market, just like any other. Like, say, a vegetable market, prices depend on supply and demand and the judgement of the buyers as to whether those cabbages represent good value and can be sold later for a profit. The only difference between a cabbage auction and the sharemarket is that one is for the sale and purchase of cabbages while the other is for the sale and purchase of a part of a business.

However, regardless of what the economy or the sharemarket overall is doing, there are always sectors and industries which are performing, as well as individual companies. To succeed on the sharemarket, it is not necessary for the market overall to be performing. Clearly this helps, but it is not essential.

To establish the quality of a company you need to look at four things:

INDUSTRY SECTOR

The area of business that a company operates in is obviously crucial. However, you will find that over time certain sectors will come in and go out of fashion – one year conglomerates are in, the next year tourism companies, which are then replaced by utilities. There is often good reason for this waxing and waning of popularity – tourism may lose out as the Kiwi dollar gains value and retailers might come into fashion when tax cuts are announced and consumer spending is set to rise.

In my view it is often best to stay away from the extremes. There are industries which will always be difficult (mining shares immediately spring to mind, but so too do airline companies). Highly fashionable companies one year are likely to be highly unfashionable the next – boom leads almost inevitably to bust.

> **Boom leads almost inevitably to bust.**

Instead it is usually better to go more heavily into industries which keep producing and selling in good times and bad – telecommunications, retail, utilities, food manufacturers. They are still subject to economic cycles, but not the whims of fashion.

In addition, industries which are difficult for competitors to enter are good. Even though a large proportion of Telecom's share value is made up of goodwill (which would normally encourage competition) this is not an industry which is easy to get into.

ASSETS

Companies with good assets make good profits. Those with old or outdated assets don't. This is mostly common sense – a new fully-automated bread bakery will do better than an old one requiring high staffing levels; a new fleet of trucks is better than old ones. Some companies have unique assets which would be difficult for a competitor to duplicate – Telecom has a large network and Baycorp has a huge database. Such assets are not just valuable in themselves but also have a long-term value in discouraging competitors.

The area that can be somewhat difficult is that of intangible assets like brands, computer software programmes, licences, franchise agreements and concessions – which are difficult to put a value on but nevertheless are essential to the business. For example, what value is the brand 'Steinlager' to Lion Nathan? The recipe itself would be of limited value (the beer could be duplicated so closely that few would know) but the name, logo and brand are surely valuable in winning sales. Licences to run a business in a National Park or to land planes in other countries, or a master franchise agreement to run KFC outlets in New Zealand may not be tangible assets but do nevertheless have a value in running a business.

LEADERSHIP AND MANAGEMENT

A strong board of directors who have a clear vision for their company, backed up by a team of good managers, is clearly important. The leadership and management functions are separate – leadership is concerned with vision and direction while management is more about day-to-day concerns and efficiency of operation. I have never been very keen on companies which are overly dominated by accountants and merchant bankers. While the financial and deal-making skills that these people bring are a necessary part of the mix, so too are management skills. Management efficiency comes from people experienced in the day-to-day running of a company, not deal-making or balance sheet juggling. Entrepreneurial deal-making is important in certain phases of most companies' lives but good solid line management is required for the long term. These two quite different skills are not always found in the same people.

NATURE OF EARNINGS

The profits of a company are not necessarily related to its cashflow. It is quite possible to have big reported profits but low cashflow and vice versa. This is brought about by such things as depreciation rates, amortisations and equity earnings from subsidiary or partly owned companies. It is sometimes more relevant to compare price to cashflow rather than earnings (companies now publish their statements of cashflows with their accounts). Profits in cash and good cashflow generally are preferable to book profits.

The other aspect of earnings and profits is how sustainable they are. Some companies derive all of their profits from good, ongoing businesses. Others take a large part of their profits from one-off deals for which there is no guarantee of a repeat. Abnormal items which appear in a company's profit statements should be substantially ignored. Profits from the sale of a company asset or of part of its business are not likely to recur year after year. Investors look for sustainable profits and value shares on these, not on the basis of one-off windfalls. A newspaper/magazine publisher or retailer has earnings which are far more preferable to those of a merchant banker or 'investment' company. The market will often rate such companies accordingly, giving the investment company a substantially lower P:E than a publisher.

Risers usually keep rising.

Clearly you want to be able to pick up quality companies as early as possible, before their earnings and share price have started to rise. This of course is not easy – anything good is telegraphed through the market, quickly causing its share price to jump.

However, do remember that risers usually keep rising. If a share jumps in price you ought not curse because you have 'missed it' and then ignore it. Many quality shares keep rising strongly for years.

One strategy to follow is to buy all new listings which come onto the market. Nearly all of these have listed at prices above their issue price, there having been very few exceptions to this in recent years. This requires a good, ongoing relationship with a sharebroker so that you get a firm allocation of new issues. However, although new issues might generally start their listed lives very well, not all carry on. There have been many instances of companies that have listed on the sharemarket giving good immediate profits but which have then languished or worse (LWR and Shotover Jet are in this category). While taking profits from a new listing (it is called 'staging') might be a good idea, if you are wanting to hold for the long term, quality rules.

Gear – But With Care

▼ ▼ ▼ ▼

*'Gearing is simply borrowing money
to buy investments.'*

GEARING IS SIMPLY BORROWING MONEY TO BUY investments. It has variously received credit (or discredit) for creating incredible riches and for the Crashes of 1929 and of 1987. It has helped people with nothing to luxury in a couple of years, and been the cause of ruin and suicide for others. It is truly a sword with two edges, able to cut both ways.

> **Those with greater investment experience and skill will definitely want to increase their gains by borrowing.**

Although as shall be seen gearing is risky, those with greater investment experience and skill will definitely want to increase their gains by borrowing.

There is a right way to gear into investments and a wrong way. If you can learn to use borrowing properly and you are a good investor it will turn success into super-success.

Gearing has had something of a bad press. The people who have had problems with gearing have had them less because they borrowed to buy investments but more because they have made poor investment decisions. The gearing has simply magnified the bad decision.

In fact all really successful investors have used gearing to achieve their success. Quite simply, the risk and reward continuum is stretched further out by gearing – those whose investment decisions are mostly good increase their gains by gearing while those whose decisions are mostly bad increase their losses. If you make good investment decisions you should be backing yourself by gearing up and leveraging your success.

The first thing to look at is what makes gearing so attractive. Borrowing money to buy investments allows you to buy more of that investment than you could otherwise afford. If you take a very positive view of a particular investment (and if you are confident in that view), borrowing to buy as much (or as many) as you can makes sense (provided of course that you are proved right in that very positive assessment).

Americans call gearing 'leverage' and either term is acceptable in New Zealand. By gearing up (or leveraging) your funds you will benefit from the appreciation of a bigger asset (or more of them) than you could by simply using the cash that you have available.

Let's look at an example of an investor who has $50,000 to invest. After careful analysis she identifies an investment which she is confident will appreciate in value. She has two alternatives:

Alternative 1: She buys investments worth $50,000 and waits. Six years later the asset has doubled in value and is now worth $100,000. Her profit is $50,000-a 100% gain in six years. This is good – but look at what happens if she gears up her funds to buy more of the same investment.

Alternative 2: She uses her $50,000 cash as a deposit and borrows $100,000 to buy investments worth $150,000. Again she waits and six years later her investment has doubled to $300,000 – a $150,000 profit. Her return on her $50,000 is 300% – not just good, but spectacular.

But gearing up also carries risks. If her analysis is wrong and she buys a poor investment which drops in value by 30% (from $150,000 to $105,000), she has lost $45,000 – nearly her total funds. On the other hand if she had not borrowed and simply invested $50,000 which then drops 30% she will have lost only $15,000 – a serious enough loss, but one that is probably sustainable. Gearing does multiply your gains but it also multiplies your losses.

▼ SPECIAL NOTE: INTERNAL RATE OF RETURN

The internal rate of return is the return that you receive from the cash that you have put into an investment after all costs (eg, interest). As such, the internal rate of return takes the effect of gearing into account and is in fact hugely affected by borrowings, both on the upside and the downside.

The internal rate of return is calculated by taking the total profit from an investment (both capital and income) and then subtracting any expenses (interest, tax, management fees). This net profit is then divided by the total cash that was originally invested.

$$irr = \frac{Profit}{Cash\ Invested} \times 100$$

For example, someone buys an investment for $50,000 which doubles over 6 years to $100,000 – her internal rate of return is 100%.

$$irr = \frac{\$50,000}{\$50,000} \times 100 = 100\%$$

However, if she had geared up by borrowing $100,000 and purchased an investment for $150,000 and that investment doubled to $300,000 her profit would be $150,000. Her internal rate of return would be:

$$irr = \frac{\$150,000}{\$50,000} \times 100 = 300\%$$

These two examples include both the gain from reinvested income as well as the capital growth and are after any costs (eg, interest). When everything is accounted for, you get a measure of the total net return that you have received on the amount of your own cash utilised.

However, these examples are simplistic – they only tell part of the story. The other part of the story is the cashflow – both income and outgoings. Any geared investment will often have both. The outgoings are interest on borrowings, the income will be rent, dividends or possibly interest.

Some geared investments start off with a cashflow deficit – ie, the outgoings are greater than the income. This is because the cash yield from investments is usually lower initially than the interest that is paid and because most people put relatively little of their own cash into the investment and borrow a relatively large amount.

The example above had someone borrowing $100,000 and using $50,000 of her own money. If we assumed that she had purchased shares with a dividend yield of 6% and was paying 10% interest on her borrowings, the numbers would look like this:

Income	
$150,000 at 6%	$9000 pa

Outgoings	
$100,000 at 10%	$10,000 pa
Cashflow deficit	($1000 pa)

This deficit will need to be made up from the investor's other income. Provided that she has structured her affairs correctly, this $1000 loss will be able to be offset against her other income for tax purposes, thus giving her a tax refund. Nevertheless, tax refund or not, cash will need to be found to ensure her lender gets paid.

> **Gearing has as much effect on the income side as it does on the capital.**

Moreover, it will not need to be paid just once; it will need to be paid continuously until either the income rises, the outgoings fall or the investment is sold.

Gearing has as much effect on the income side as it does on the capital. This is because if the capital value has either grown or declined it will be because the income has grown or declined. There is a double whammy – either a very good double whammy or a very bad one.

If we go back to the example in Alternative 2 and look at what happens if the investor has a 100% rise or a 30% fall in her investments, we can put in the income and outgoing figures. The assumption is that the income remains at a 6% yield and the borrowings stay at 10% pa.

Scenario 1:	**The investment rises by 100%**	
Initial value	$150,000 at 6%	$9000 pa
Borrowings	$100,000 at 10%	($10,000 pa)
Cash deficit		($1000 pa)
New value	$300,000 at 6%	$18,000 pa
Borrowings	$100,000 at 10%	($10,000 pa)
Cash surplus		$8000 pa

Not only has the investor got a 300% capital profit, she also has $8000 of income each year after she has paid the interest on her borrowings. Given that she only invested $50,000, she is doing very well!

Scenario 2:   The investment falls by 30%

Initial value	$150,000 at 6%	$9000 pa
Borrowings	$100,000 at 10%	($10,000 pa)
Cash deficit		($1000 pa)
New value	$105,000 at 6%	$6300 pa
Borrowings	$100,000 at 10%	($10,000 pa)
Cash deficit		($3700 pa)

Along with her capital loss of $45,000 is an increased cash deficit of $3700 every year. The investor obviously believed she could manage the initial cash deficit of $1000 pa (around $20 per week) from her other income but now she needs to find $3700 pa (over $70 per week). At this level, life might start to look a bit grim!

Of course the investment might fall more than 30% – it could collapse altogether. Regardless of what happens to the value and income from the investment, the borrowings carry on. Frequently the numbers are much bigger than this (especially for property investors) and of course the income might stop altogether, either because you lose a tenant or a company stops paying dividends.

It is for this reason that the quality rule is particularly important for investors who are gearing up to buy investments. You really do need to make the right investment decisions when you are gearing yourself up. The only real safeguards are to either buy top quality assets (good sustainable income) or to buy into one of the leveraged sharemarket investments like warrants and options which are structured deliberately to limit the investor's downside.

▼ SPECIAL NOTE: TWO-STAGE DECISION

For many people investment is really a two-stage process.
▼ What should I buy?
▼ Should I gear up to buy it?

The first question is the more difficult. However, once that is answered the second question needs to be tackled. It would be possible to make a case for saying that the answer to question 2 should always be 'yes!' – you should always gear up when buying shares or property. After all, if you are not confident that you are making a good investment, buying something which will rise in value and perform, why are you buying it in the first place? If you have properly analysed the market and the investment you should back yourself to be right.

> **If you have properly analysed the market and the investment you should back yourself to be right.**

However, things are seldom that simple. First of all, there are degrees of confidence in any investment decision that you take. Second, your financial or personal position may or may not suit geared investment. Third, you may not be able to carry a temporary loss or cash deficit as your investment shows some volatility.

The really attractive thing about a two-stage investment process is that it forces you to at least consider gearing each time you invest, rather than unconsciously and unthinkingly borrowing or not borrowing. Of course some people will have no choice but to gear up if they are going to invest. Property investors nearly always need to borrow to buy their investments – few of us have the hundred of thousands (or millions) of dollars that are necessary in cash. However, when you do have a choice (as you often do with equities), that choice should be exercised logically and rationally each time you invest.

Note that the interest costs associated with borrowing to buy investments are tax deductible. It does not matter what security is used to borrow; provided you borrow for the purpose of investing to obtain assessable income (rents, interest and dividends) the cost of the borrowings can be claimed. Therefore if you use your house as security to borrow to buy a rental property, or your personal credit card to buy shares, the interest cost is a deductible expense.

Any overall income losses may be offset against any other taxable income that you have (eg, salary or business profits). However, capital losses cannot be claimed off tax unless you are a trader. If you are a trader (rather than an investor) you will be buying investments with the intention and purpose of selling them at a profit. This will mean that the capital profits that you make will be taxable but the losses will be deductible. On the other hand, investors who purchase assets for their income and long-term growth pay no tax on their capital profits but cannot offset their capital losses against other assessable income.

Because of the tax treatment of borrowing and the fact that there is no capital gains tax in New Zealand, there are many investors who use gearing in an attempt to swap taxable income for non-taxable capital gain. This was extremely popular in the 1970s and 1980s when we had high taxation and very high inflation giving (seemingly in hindsight) a guarantee of capital growth in both property and shares. Although neither of those two factors are as compelling as they once were, there are nevertheless many investors today who arrange their affairs to achieve the same result.

> **Gearing has the effect of exchanging taxable income for capital growth.**

Gearing has the effect of exchanging taxable income for capital growth because the cash yield from investments is usually lower than the cost of borrowing. For example, the cash yield from the investment might be 6% while the cost of borrowings is 10%.

Unless you provide a large deposit and borrow very little it is in fact quite difficult to borrow to buy an investment and retain a cash surplus.

If we look again at the investor with $50,000 to invest, if she simply invested the funds at 6% without borrowing (Alternative 1) she would have had a good capital gain (tax free) plus some income on which she would pay tax. However, if she had geared herself up to buy $150,000 worth of investments, her tax-free capital gain is not just good, it is exceptional. Her taxable income is, however, quite different. Assuming that she borrowed her $100,000 at 10% her income in the early years would be very low – in fact in the first year she actually has a deficit of $1000 (see page 145). Ultimately she will have very high taxable income – after 6 years when the investment has doubled she will have $8000 of taxable income.

There are many investors who keep borrowing more money as their income and the value of their investments rise. They use the new value and higher income to borrow more funds so that they stay in a low – or no-income position. This is called pyramiding. Some investors have become very, very rich from this continual borrowing process. Because they have purchased the right assets they have been able to continue to lever the growth in value that they have obtained, becoming super-rich without ever paying a cent of tax.

There are also those who have gone bankrupt doing it. These are people who may have been successful early on with their investment decisions but who keep borrowing, keep getting bigger, until they purchase the wrong thing. With this continual gearing-up process, you are only as good as your last deal, be that a great success or a horrendous mistake. I believe that you should use your capital and income growth to lower your overall gearing ratio over time. This means that instead of continuing to borrow so that your borrowings are, say, 66% of your asset value, you buy (and therefore borrow) a little less so that the percentage reduces.

▼ SPECIAL NOTE: NEGATIVE GEARING

Borrowing to the extent of having a cash deficit is called negative gearing. It is a term mostly used by property investors but works just as well for those buying shares.

I am no great fan of excessive negative gearing. It is an arrangement which needs to be set up with great thought and care. To gear up is one thing – to gear up with a large cash deficit is quite another. To go into a negative gearing arrangement you need to be confident of two things:

▼ **That you have bought good investments.** In essence, you need to be able to back the investment that you have bought to outperform the financing costs. This requires skill and good judgement.

▼ **That you have very secure income from other sources.** This income may come from your job, your business or from other investments. You cannot be reliant (without good cause) on the income from the investment increasing to cover the cash deficit. It may be that the property you are buying has a rent review coming up which is likely to be higher or the company that you are investing in is to increase its dividend, in which case you might not need to rely on other income. However, you would be most unwise to be reliant on general growth to cover the deficit in the near term.

Without security of income and confidence in your ability to pick quality investments you should arrange your investments so that you start off with a very small (or no) cash deficit. This means being very selective – you can no longer buy any old property or any old portfolio of shares.

There are many different types of gearing arrangements – everything from margin trading to property purchases. There are even people who have geared investment but are not aware of it. For example, if you have any borrowings (home mortgage, credit card, etc) and you also have investments, you are in effect borrowing for those investments. The point is you do have a choice – you could sell the investments and repay all or part of the debt. Because you don't do that, your investments are carrying your borrowings.

In fact, for many people, having personal debt (usually the home mortgage) together with investments is not very sensible. Generally the cost of the mortgage interest will not be matched by tax-paid returns from your investments. If you are paying 10% for your mortgage, you are paying that with tax paid dollars (the mortgage is not a deductible expense unless you took it out to buy investments). To match that you would need to get a return from your investment of 15% before tax. That sort of return is not easily achieved except by investors who are especially skilled. It is most unlikely to be achieved by balanced funds with a spread of investments such as those that are offered for superannuation.

This situation changes quite quickly, however, when you are borrowing specifically to invest (as opposed to simply investing while you have a mortgage on the house). The reason that it changes so quickly is tax – borrowing to invest means the interest is tax-deductible.

Although the principle of gearing remains the same for all three investment types, the details change quite a lot.

INTEREST-EARNING DEPOSITS

No thinking person would borrow money to put into bonds or bank deposits – the returns are too low and are all taxable. Nevertheless there are people who are in exactly that position (they do it unthinkingly). Those who have a mortgage and who have money in the bank are in precisely that position. This is one of the least sensible financial arrangements that can be imagined. Effectively you are lending money to the bank and paying tax on the interest received. The bank is then putting its profit margin on (perhaps $1\frac{1}{2}$-2%) and lending it back to you. To add insult to injury you have to pay your mortgage interest with tax-paid dollars.

> **No thinking person would borrow money to put into bonds or bank deposits.**

A better way to arrange things is to have a revolving credit facility (which works like an overdraft). If you have such a facility you do not need to hold cash against an emergency – instead you have a line of credit which you can draw on.

PROPERTY

Property is the most popular investment to gear up (although not necessarily the easiest). From a lender's point of view, property provides good security because it tends to at least hold its value, there is a fairly well worn legal pathway in the event of the borrower defaulting and because if it does come to repossession the property will be there to repossess – although possibly not in the condition that the lender would like!

It is popular to borrow on property because few people have enough cash to buy properties without mortgaging, because of the high returns that have traditionally come from property, and because of the tax efficiency.

Property is an interesting investment because it can give anything from high income with moderate capital growth to low/no income with high growth – or you can fit anywhere on that spectrum that you choose. Where you fit depends to some extent on the type of property that you buy (some are higher yielding than others) but to a greater extent your type of return will be set by the amount that you gear your property purchase. The greater your borrowings the lower your cash return (or yield) will be and the higher capital growth will be, and vice versa. This is certainly so in the early years of your investment, but it is likely to change as capital values and rents rise or decline (see graph opposite).

Many people in New Zealand have purchased rental properties using their house (as well as the rental property) as security and borrowing 100% of the purchase price. This almost certainly means that the property will be negatively geared (and therefore carry a cash deficit) and they 'subsidise' the property out of their income (they see this as a sort of enforced savings plan). The idea is that over time (perhaps 20 years) they will repay the borrowings and so

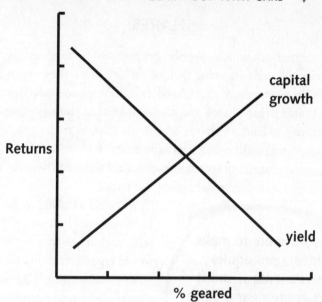

can retire with a mortgage-free house giving them good income to live off which should rise with (if not slightly ahead) of inflation.

For this to work, I believe that there needs to be very careful selection of the property to be purchased. Investors who put none of their own cash in are 100% geared and accordingly very exposed, especially in the early years. The days are long gone when you could borrow to buy any property in New Zealand and do well. Any 100% geared property investment would almost certainly want to be in one of our major centres which has population growth and a diversified economy, not in some small town economically dependent on its sawmill or freezing works.

The major disadvantage for property gearing is that the numbers are so big. For most people purchasing property, the size of the purchase will be large relative to their other assets. Mistakes (particularly ones involving loss of tenants or income) are therefore serious or even financially fatal. You might be able to borrow to buy a small amount of shares but you cannot generally do that with property; it nearly always involves numbers with at least six figures. The greatest care and thought is therefore needed.

SHARES

The degree to which people borrow to buy shares is still surprisingly high. It is true that we no longer have the excesses of the 1980s when people mortgaged their houses and loaded up their credit cards to buy shares, and banks and finance houses competed vigorously to lend on shares or provide margin trading facilities. However, there are other (perhaps more sophisticated) ways of making leveraged equity investments and some of these are now very popular in spite of being less obvious.

It is in fact easier to gear up to buy shares than property (although there are people who would try to contradict this). In fact, as shall be seen, it is possible to make leveraged equity investments without ever going near a bank manager nor directly paying a cent in interest.

> **It is possible to make leveraged equity investments without ever going near a bank manager nor directly paying a cent in interest.**

The most simple and least sophisticated way to gear up to buy shares is to borrow on the security of something else, probably the family home. Few lenders now regard share scrip as great security and so will not therefore advance much against the shares that you purchase. You need to find something else to use as security and the family home will probably be the cheapest and easiest. Of course by borrowing against the family home, you put your house directly at risk. This will of course be of concern and will no doubt cause many to reconsider gearing to buy shares or at least provide some discipline to ensure the purchase of the right shares. However, you should understand that whatever you put up as security, you will in any case be required to personally guarantee the facility which will put all of your assets at risk. So when you borrow on a property to buy shares and all goes wrong, if the

> **By borrowing against the family home, you put your house directly at risk.**

lender is not paid in full out of the sale of the property they will ultimately be able to force you to sell other assets (including the family home) to make up the shortfall.

The decision therefore is not so much what to use for security but rather what to buy and whether or not you should be borrowing and gearing up.

MARGIN TRADING

Margin trading used to be the most popular way to gear into shares. Now with other securities like options and warrants it has declined in use although some financial institutions and sharebrokers do offer and promote it. Margin trading becomes popular in times of good sharemarket performance. It does have an advantage over options and warrants in that it allows you to purchase any share, rather than only the one where options and warrants are offered. In addition it allows you to own these shares outright, for as long as you want, not just for the limited life of options and warrants.

Margin trading is usually done through lending institutions specialising in lending on share purchases, or through a share-broker who offers the service. After becoming a client of the company and signing a contract you can make purchases of any shares you wish, provided that you put up the required deposit. Typically you would need to provide a 35% deposit for blue chip shares, 45% deposit for second line shares and perhaps 50% deposit for very volatile shares. This deposit is called your 'margin'. The balance of the purchase price is lent to you by the lender and you will pay monthly interest on it. You will receive the dividends which will go some way towards helping pay the interest.

Once the shares have been purchased, the lending institution will hold the share certificates as security. Sometimes the lending institution will actually purchase the shares for you and hold them in its own name. Although the only thing that the lender takes for security is the share scrip, you are personally liable for the total amount of the borrowings. In the event that the shares that you have borrowed on collapsed completely to nil value, you would need to find all of the borrowed money and repay the lender out of other assets. This is why so many people were badly hurt (even bankrupted) in the crashes of 1929 and 1987 (both times when there was a lot of margin trading).

The deposit that you pay (your margin) must be maintained at all times, even if the share price falls. The lender will require that you keep at least the same amount of equity throughout. If the shares that you have purchased fall by a significant amount you will find yourself on a margin call. This unpleasant experience is a call from your lender to add to your margin (or deposit) so that you retain the same percentage of equity in the shares. If you cannot meet the margin call the lender will sell the shares at the best price she can get in sufficient quantities to meet the margin call.

If on the other hand the shares rise, you can use the additional equity created by that rise to buy more shares. If there are a lot of people buying on a margin, this is self-fulfilling – as the shares rise traders can buy more shares which drives them higher which means they can buy more . . . until, of course it busts.

With margin trading, there are four main rules:

▼ Try to time your purchases when the shares are on a rise (easier said than done!) to avoid a margin call.

▼ Always have enough cash on hand to meet a margin call.

▼ Be prepared to sell quickly (at a loss if necessary) if you get it wrong.

▼ Do not gear to the maximum allowable – always have a buffer.

FUTURES CONTRACTS

There are a few people who obtain their exposure to shares by buying futures contracts based on the NZSE index.

The index is a sort of synthetic or artificial portfolio of shares made up of the leading 40 companies in proportion to their size. The portfolio will contain, say, 27% Telecom, 13% Carter Holt Harvey, 8% Fletcher Energy, etc.

On the Futures Exchange, each point on the index is valued at $25. Therefore if the index is at 2350, the contract is worth $58,750

(2350 x $25). In buying one contract on the index at 2350 you are in effect promising to buy a share portfolio valued at $58,750.

That is all a futures contract is – a contract (or promise) to buy (or sell) this synthetic, artificial share portfolio at some point in the future at an agreed price. Normally futures contracts do not go beyond 12 months and are more common for 3 or 6 months meaning that you cannot use futures to get share value growth beyond that time. Contracts are for a stated period of time when they must be closed out.

Of course for everyone buying a synthetic portfolio, there must also be a seller. There are people who, taking the view that the share-market will fall, sell the index short. Those are usually either specu-lators taking a gamble or people holding a physical portfolio who want to hedge their position. The price of the contracts will be set by the market, according to how many people want to buy the index and how many want to sell. Normally the futures contracts will trade at a value close to the actual sharemarket index. However, there is often a premium or discount depending upon the market's view. If the futures market thinks that the sharemarket is likely to rise, the futures contracts will trade at a premium in anticipation of that rise. If it thinks it will fall, it will trade at a discount.

Futures contracts are highly geared (which is the attraction to speculators in particular). When you contract to buy a synthetic share portfolio valued at $58,750 you will only pay a deposit (or margin) of 5% – you do not need to pay the balance until the contract is closed out. This is a very high gearing ratio. However, just like margin trading, you must retain your equity even when the market moves against you. If for example the market fell by 100 points, this would be a loss of $2500 for you (each point is valued at $25). You would then get a margin call – your broker would ask you to restore your margin.

You can, of course, if you wish, provide more than that 5% as a deposit. If you do not want to be so highly geared you can simply put more cash into the contract.

Futures markets are quite sophisticated and can move very quickly. There is a great deal of detail and jargon which you would need to know to operate successfully. Brokers and others in the market frequently speak very quickly in their own peculiar language. They seldom seem to have time to explain things carefully or in English. However, in spite of the rather frightening nature of the market, it is a valid means to invest in shares for those who have the skill and want a leveraged investment.

OPTIONS AND WARRANTS

The growth in popularity of these securities in New Zealand has been remarkable in recent years (it is even more so in Australia). Although there are some relatively minor technical differences between options and warrants, they are similar in principle and in the way they work. Both give a very good easy way to lever sharemarket investments. Their popularity has been based on the fact that they are easy to understand, easy to access and can give very good returns with a minimum of risk. As such they are probably the best way to gear up share purchases for most smaller private investors and have been quite heavily promoted by issuing financial institutions.

When you purchase the warrant, your loss is limited to that purchase price.

A warrant or an option is a piece of paper giving the right to buy a certain share on or before a certain date at a certain price. Although the warrant gives you the right to do this, you are not obligated to buy the share, meaning that a considerable part of the risk is taken out for you. In effect, when you purchase the warrant, your loss is limited to that purchase price.

For example, you purchase an option for 10¢ giving you the right to buy a Telecom share in two years time for 900¢. If Telecom does not reach or exceed that value within two years, your option is worthless – you have lost your 10¢. But you have only lost your 10¢ – nothing else. You are not obligated to purchase the share because it is trading at 720¢. If you were obligated to buy the share you would carry a major loss.

On the other hand Telecom might trade up to 950¢. You could exercise your option and buy the share at 900¢ and sell it immediately to make a 50¢ profit (less the 10¢ price of the option). That is a very good return, given your initial outlay.

There is an element of gambling here – there is a chase between the share price and the clock. The gamble is largely about timing – will the price reach the strike price before the exercise date? However, it is a gamble with a limited downside – unlike most geared investments, with options and warrants you can only lose the amount of your initial investment. When you borrow to buy property or shares your risk is far greater than simply your deposit – it is as much as the total borrowings.

Most options and warrants are traded before their exercise date. The models used to price and value them on the market can be very complicated but generally the options will move up or down with the value of the underlying head share. Warrants and options are usually very volatile – their value changes far more in percentage terms than does the head share. For example, in 1997 the Deutsche Bank Warrant for Fletcher Forest varied between 3¢ and 13¢ (a difference of over 400%), while the Fletcher Forest shares themselves traded between 133¢ and 242¢ (less than 100%). This volatility makes warrants and options very good for traders and speculators.

However, for investors the downside risk is only covered as long as you buy the same number of warrants as you would have bought shares. This means not purchasing the same dollar value of options as you would have bought shares. For example, an investor has $20,000 to invest. The shares that he wants to buy, ABC Ltd, are trading at 500¢ and the options are trading at 40¢. The investor could put all of his money into buying 4000 shares at 500¢. On the other hand he could buy 50,000 options at 40¢. However, if he did this he would not have limited his downside risk – he could lose his entire $20,000 because that is the amount he has put in. In fact, given the volatility of warrants and the fact that there is a race against time for the head shares to reach a certain level, the investor has not just failed to cover his risk but has increased it.

What the investor should consider doing instead is to purchase 4000 options, the same number of options as he was going to buy shares. That way he still has the benefit of owning 4000 shares (which benefit increases markedly once the shares have gone through the exercise price) and his risk is limited to 40¢ on each share. These warrants will have cost the investor just $1600, meaning that $18,400 of his funds remain unspent. This money could be invested elsewhere, perhaps simply put in the bank to get interest.

There is a great temptation to put all of your funds into options – to control 50,000 shares instead of 4000 shares. When tempted, however, remember the effect of gearing when things go wrong and recognise that by putting all of your money in, you have not properly used the ability of warrants to limit your risk.

> **Those with skill, experience and judgement will gear themselves up, leveraging their success.**

There are many different sorts of warrants and options. Some are issued by the company itself, but most are organised by banks. Some are able to be sold on the share-market, some on more informal secondary markets and some need to be held right through to the exercise date. Some warrants are based on just one company's share (eg, Carter Holt Harvey or Air New Zealand) while others are based on a basket of shares. There will continue to be new types of warrants issued and promoted.

Borrowing to buy investments does (and should!) frighten new investors. However, those with skill, experience and judgement will gear themselves up, leveraging their success into greater success. Timing will always be important periods of great speculative frenzy are not good times to gear, even though to a large extent they may be driven by it.

Time in the Market
and Timing the Market
are Both Important

▼ ▼ ▼ ▼

*'There is no reason why you
cannot time the market well
and then stay with it for a
long period of time.'*

MUCH HAS BEEN WRITTEN AND SPOKEN ABOUT THE importance of going into a market and staying there. That you buy into some investments and stay with them is regarded as being far more important than trying to buy the dips and sell the peaks. In fact, it is asserted that it is impossible to time markets anyway, so don't bother trying – just buy at any time and stay with it.

This has been repeated so many times that it has become a truism, a matter of investment lore. As such it is seldom examined.

I think that part of this idea is true and part is untrue. The statements in magazines like '. . . it is futile to try to time the market' or from fund managers that 'time in the markets not timing the market is a wise strategy for the individual investor' are to some extent both defeatist and misleading. The fund manager making the statement is perfectly confident that it can time the markets – it seems to believe that the individual cannot. What the fund manager seems to be saying is 'don't you worry yourselves about this – leave it to us'. I can see no reason why private investors cannot time the market and every reason why they should try. They will not be able to time the market minutely, picking the absolute perfect time to buy or sell – no one can. However, they can certainly look at the big picture and recognise times which are better to buy (or sell) in than others.

The truth is, of course, that time in the market and timing the market are both important – and they are not mutually exclusive. There is no reason why you cannot time the market well and then stay with it for a long period of time. Provided you do not try to call accurately every market movement (and arrange your finances so that you are dependent on being right), you should watch for the signs to be in or to be out.

Ignoring the ups and downs of any market will give you approximately an average return.

Time in the market will give you the bulk of your return, but timing the market even reasonably well will give a performance above average – something most investors are looking for. Ignoring the ups and downs of any market will give you approximately an average return. That return is still likely to be good, assuming that our bond, equity and property markets continue to perform as they have in the past, but timing the market in a broad way should give you returns that are not just good but excellent. Unquestionably it is important (indeed it is most important) that you buy quality investments and stay with them. But surely that does not mean you should stay with the same allocation of assets or the same individual shares, properties or bonds for very long periods of time, ignoring entirely what is happening?

Timing the big trends in the market is like the icing on the cake. It is a way to beat the average or benchmark.

Much of the decision as to whether or not to try to time the market will depend on the type of investor that you are. The longer the time that you are investing for, the less important is timing. People who are investing for 30 years are far less concerned with timing than those looking at five years. Skills and investment aptitude are also important – those with them are likely to try to apply what they know and seek out investments which will out-perform the average in the near term. Those without them should be happy investing without the worry of the noise of the market, staying in for the long term.

Regardless of who you are, it is certainly true that you cannot time the market down to the day, the week or the month. If you wanted to know what is likely to happen to bond, property or equity markets in the short term you would be disappointed – it is impossible to tell. However, the bigger trends are certainly possible to pick, as shall be seen later.

Where the real danger lies is in people trying to pick the very bottom of a market to buy and the very top to sell. This leads to greedy short-term thinking which is likely to be self-defeating. There is a very old business saying that you should always let the other guy make a profit (another way to put it is to always leave some salt on the bread). This means not holding out for the last dollar, not trying to wait for the very top to sell, or to buy at the bottom. In fact, only one person buys at the bottom or sells at the top – given the number of people operating in the market your chance of being that person is not very good. Even trying may be counterproductive as you hold on to squeeze the last cent out of an investment only to have it reverse and move against you.

Sir Robert Muldoon was outspoken in his beliefs that the 1986-87 sharemarket boom was going to bust. He was laughed at when he said it. Even after the Crash which he had predicted finally happened, people gave him little credit, saying that Sir Robert had simply kept saying the same thing over and over again and if you keep doing that for long enough you are bound to be proven right eventually.

Looking back, this is extremely unfair. Sir Robert did call it correctly. He may not have got the timing right exactly (who could?) but he certainly recognised that there was little value left in the market; that P:E ratios were too high, dividend yields too low (or non-existent) and earnings themselves too fragile. There is no doubt that Sir Robert timed the market properly when he called to sell. Even though the market went higher after that, people would have been better off selling at that time than waiting.

You may not be able to call markets on a short-term basis but it is possible to do so if you are not greedy and look to the longer term.

TIME IN THE MARKET

Time in the market is the most important factor in investment success. This is for two reasons:

1. **The compounding effect of money.** Everyone knows that the returns you receive (interest, rentals, dividends and even capital growth) get you even more returns if you reinvest them. The thing which surprises many people is the extent to which this happens. Returns added back into capital to get more returns mean that although

> **Time in the market is the most important factor in investment success.**

your capital rises slowly at first, gradually it picks up to rise strongly, then spectacularly.

One of the best examples of the effect of compounding is the story of a Persian prince who was purchasing a horse. In response to 'how much?' the horse trader took out a chess board with 64 squares. His payment would be for the prince to put one grain of wheat on the first square, two on the second square, four on the third square . . . doubling the amount each time until all the squares were used. The prince agreed – and lost his kingdom. All the wheat in Persia was not enough to cover the last square.

Such is the effect of compounding and doubling your wealth. This doubling will be fast or slow depending on just one thing – the return that you get. The higher the return, the quicker your wealth will double.

The Rule of 72 says that 72 divided by the percentage returns you get will give you the number of years it takes for your capital to double. For example, if you are getting a return of 6% it will take 12 years for your capital to double ($72 \div 6 = 12$) or if you are getting a 12% return it will take 6 years for your return to double ($72 \div 12 = 6$).

Going into the market and staying there allows time to act on your money. That does not work if you take it out or stop investing it. You need to keep it in there, avoiding any temptation to spend it.

2. **Trying to time the market too much may lead you to be out of the market at just the wrong time.** Markets often move in big jumps, both up and down. Miss out on some of those jumps and you can lose much of your return. A bear market usually has more up days than down days – it is just that the down days are bigger. It is certainly true that over long periods of time our property and sharemarkets have risen and have provided on average very good investment media. There is no doubt in my mind that you should take advantage of these investments even if you never aim to achieve anything more than the average. You are far better to

get an average investment return than to do nothing and so get no return.

It is notoriously difficult to buy and sell markets, trading the short-term rises. I can easily go back and show how rich you could have been if you had purchased share A at 79¢; sold it 2 weeks later at 92¢; put the proceeds into share B at 142¢; sold it 3 months later for 185¢; put the proceeds into share C at 42¢; sold it 6 weeks later at 67¢ . . . in a couple of years you would have been fabulously rich. However, although I can easily do this sort of trading looking backwards, I cannot do it looking forwards. I can't pick these short-term shifts. What is likely to happen is that I would make a mistake and be wiped out, or become impatient when the share did not move and sell too soon. I may well find that I am not in the market at the very time that I want to be in – that is at the time of a major upwards shift.

The market moves in large jumps when new information appears or something (perhaps in politics or the economy) happens. Very often there is a lag time – and then a rapid catch-up. When that catch-up will come is anybody's guess. If you are not in at the time, you miss out.

A fund manager once produced the following figures showing the returns that an investor would get if he invested at different times. Both investors invest $5,000 each year. The investor on the left (a seemingly hopeless case) invests each year at the absolute wrong time – just when the market has reached its annual high point. The investor on the right (a brilliant fellow) times the market perfectly, putting his money in at the market's annual low point.

This is how they do:

Date of market high	Cumulative investment $	Investment value on 31 December $	Date of market low	Cumulative investment $	Investment value on 31 December $
11 Jan 1965	5000	4379	23 Dec 1965	5000	5000
14 Apr 1966	10,000	8906	8 Nov 1966	10,000	10,062
5 Jan 1967	15,000	12,797	11 Nov 1967	15,000	14,416
8 Nov 1968	20,000	22,814	19 Jan 1968	20,000	27,225
23 Dec 1969	25,000	31,419	13 Jan 1969	25,000	37,279
8 Jan 1970	30,000	32,432	24 Nov 1970	30,000	38,417
7 Jan 1971	35,000	36,153	22 Sep 1971	35,000	42,500
22 Dec 1972	40,000	48,343	12 Apr 1972	40,000	57,063
6 July 1973	45,000	51,404	7 Dec 1973	45,000	61,023
21 Mar 1974	50,000	44,084	5 Nov 1974	50,000	53,477
22 May 1975	55,000	53,665	14 Jan 1975	55,000	65,233
2 Sep 1976	60,000	60,545	5 Jan 1976	60,000	73,292
10 Jan 1977	65,000	61,615	2 Sep 1977	65,000	74,213
21 July 1978	70,000	73,937	10 Jan 1978	70,000	88,857
7 Nov 1979	75,000	86,783	23 Feb 1979	75,000	104,159
26 Nov 1980	80,000	137,692	7 Jan 1980	80,000	167,000
15 June 1981	85,000	180,792	6 Jan 1981	85,000	219,582
5 Feb 1982	90,000	157,518	1 Dec 1982	90,000	191,613
21 Dec 1983	95,000	346,500	10 Jan 1983	95,000	426,481
24 Dec 1984	100,000	395,223	14 Aug 1984	100,000	486,633
18 Dec 1985	105,000	524,170	30 Jan 1985	105,000	646,283
10 Nov 1986	110,000	1,049,141	20 Jan 1986	110,000	1,297,797
18 Sep 1987	115,000	542,444	22 Dec 1987	115,000	673,026
18 July 1988	120,000	516,330	29 Feb 1988	120,000	641,023
5 Sep 1989	125,000	563,754	4 Jan 1989	125,000	700,284
3 Jan 1990	130,000	342,903	18 Dec 1990	130,000	427,467
7 May 1991	135,000	433,712	15 Jan 1991	135,000	541,320
12 July 1992	140,000	456,527	19 Oct 1992	140,000	569,413
2 Nov 1993	145,000	642,430	21 Jan 1993	145,000	802,484
2 Feb 1994	150,000	565,902	12 Feb 1994	150,000	707,086

Total net return		$ 565,902	Total net return		$ 707,086
Average annual rate of return		10.03%	Average annual rate of return		12.97%

Both investors have, in fact done fairly well – the 'hopeless case' has returned 10.03% and has $565,000 in his bank while the 'brilliant fellow' has managed 12.97% and has $707,000 in his bank.

The difference is probably not as great as you would expect. Certainly both are far better off than if they had done nothing; time in the market has worked for both.

However, the table does not say to me that you are better off not timing the market if you can – in fact quite the opposite. Had either listened to Sir Robert Muldoon (who did seem to be able to time the market) and sold out in 1986 they would have had over $1 million. Even if they had sold out anywhere between 1985 and 1989 they would have been better off. The timing does not have to be very precise! Anywhere within a five-year period would have been better. Difficult though timing may be, it does seem to be worth trying, provided that you aim to work the big swings, not the ones that are daily, weekly or monthly.

> **The timing does not have to be very precise! Anywhere within a five-year period would have been better.**

However, as previously stated, not everyone will have the skills nor aptitude to try to outperform the market. These people will be perfectly satisfied if they can achieve the average. All they are hoping is that they do not perform like the 'hopeless case' who consistently bought at the wrong time. How can you be sure to achieve the average? The answer is dollar cost averaging.

DOLLAR COST AVERAGING

This is jargon for making regular savings or contributions into a certain market. The idea is that each period (usually each month) you make the same payment (always the same total amount of money) into the market regardless of what has happened to the market and to the price. Therefore each month you will get a different number of units or shares.

The effect of this is that it will average out the price that you have paid and will remove any issue of short-term timing of the market. The payments are made regularly. If the price has gone up you will get fewer units; if it has gone down you will get more. After some time your price paid will reflect the average price over that time, no more and no less. Your investment performance therefore will follow the market average.

In terms of the fund manager's table on page 167, your investment performance will be somewhere between 'hopeless case' and 'brilliant fellow' because there are no timing issues involved. The only difference between the returns of these two was their timing – in the case of the dollar cost averager, that timing variable has been removed.

A variation of dollar cost averaging is to put your money into an investment over a set period, perhaps 3 or 6 months. This is called 'stepping' and means that you invest your money in thirds or perhaps fifths. For example, you have $15,000 to invest. Each month for 5 months you put $3,000 into the investment. This has the effect of taking out some of the short-term timing distortions; you will tend to buy in at the average price of the last 5 months.

Dollar cost averaging does work. It is what has always happened with the contributions of very long-term investors into superannuation schemes. These keep coming out of the bank account or out of the pay packet each week, regardless of what has been happening on the investment markets.

However, there are two warnings which need to be given:

1. **Do not completely close your eyes when dollar cost averaging into an undiversified investment.** For example, you should not blindly pay in each month to just one share or property syndicate. To be so unvaried requires both eyes wide open and some concentration. Even to make regular contributions into a portfolio of only shares or only property (via some sort of managed fund) requires at least half an eye open – it would make little sense to keep pouring funds into

these if they were grossly overvalued. However, you can probably happily close both eyes if you are paying into a good diversified or balanced fund which holds a mix of all of the investment types. Such a strategy will not give spectacular returns but it is safe and steady.

2. **Do not confuse dollar cost averaging with the very silly idea of averaging down.** People 'average down' when they have purchased an investment which has then fallen in value. They buy more of the investment at the lower price so that they average the price of their investment. For example, they have purchased a share at 200¢ and the price falls to 150¢; they buy more at 150¢ so that the average is 175¢. It may well be that it is a good idea to buy more of these shares at 150¢ – if the company was properly analysed and was a good buy at 200¢, it is an even better buy at 150¢. However, it is just as likely that there is a reason for the company's share price falling; perhaps the analysis was wrong. The company needs to be reinvestigated before any further money goes in.

Simply spending time in the market to achieve average returns is good enough for many conservative and less enthusiastic investors. However, others will want to try to outperform the market by means of superior investment selection and by timing. Many will achieve that – after all, an average performance is just that; there will be people both above the average and below it.

Anyone who wants to outperform the market must learn two things – to buy in gloom and sell in boom, and value investing.

BUY IN GLOOM, SELL IN BOOM

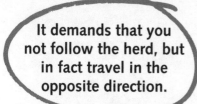

It demands that you not follow the herd, but in fact travel in the opposite direction.

This is a contrarian's approach. It demands that you not follow the herd, but in fact travel in the opposite direction, which is far harder to do than to say. While buying in gloomy times and selling in booming times is logical and rational, it requires a considerable sense of purpose, strength of character and discipline to actually do it. You need to know that what you are doing is right!

Markets are full of noise and confusion and uncertainty. Indeed, a market has to have uncertainty and disagreement – if everyone agrees the price will increase rapidly until people no longer agree. There has to be both buyers and sellers to have a market – that is, you need both optimists and pessimists, bulls and bears, those who think the market will rise and those who think it will fall.

Although there is that uncertainty, there are often times when there is general consensus one way or the other, an overwhelming number of people on one particular side. The easiest to identify examples of this in both our property and share markets were 1986 when (nearly) everyone was an optimistic buyer and 1990, when (nearly) everyone was a pessimistic seller.

We can look back with wonder and awe at people buying shares in 1986 at P:E ratios of 30 and properties with yields of 5%, and at people selling shares in 1990 at P:Es of 8 and properties on yields of 14%. We can marvel at this, even scoff if we want.

On the other hand, we can make a conscious decision to learn from it. After all, there were contrarians who sold in 1986 and people who bought in 1990. Some may have been just lucky – but others would have been principled investors, following their own precepts. That is worth thinking about. If we can use the experience gained through that period, we should be able to time our purchases and our sales next time.

▼SPECIAL NOTE: THE INVESTMENT CLOCK

The investment clock is a common way of showing how the economy in general and markets in particular work in cycles. It is a means of identifying where we are in that cycle and what you should be doing.

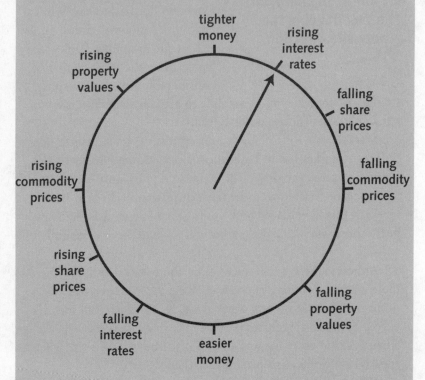

However, this is not the clock that you should set your Rolex by. It is not particularly accurate nor very reliable. Economies and markets never work out this neatly – if they did we would all know where we are and what we should be doing. Even if we could rely on it telling us what is coming up next, it would not tell us precisely when the hand was going to move.

The clock gives a broad idea of the cycles. It will not tell us the hour, let alone the minute – but it might tell us whether it is night or day. Best of all, it serves to remind us that boom follows gloom (and vice versa); that 'if it is night, then day will follow'; that no cycle lasts forever.

As an investor you are in a continual search for value or for cheap earnings. The very time when those earnings are cheapest is when that market is unfashionable. This is not necessarily so only when something major is going on like in the 1980s bull run or the bear market after the Crash – there are smaller cycles within the major swings.

Recognising these down-swings as a time to buy is not easy. The markets are full of noise – a confusing cacophony of sound with politicians, economists, public servants and experts commenting. The noise is amplified by the media. Brokers' comments each morning in the newspaper can make the previous day's trading on the sharemarket sound like a pivotal point in the history of man and the next day's trade likely to be just as dramatic. The reef fish start to look more like a cattle stampede.

Trading against this, being unfashionable, is lonely. No one likes turning up to a barbecue in formal wear by mistake. It is uncomfortable standing out in the crowd.

> **No one likes turning up to a barbecue in formal wear by mistake.**

Nor is it right to simply make a point of standing out, to always go against the crowd. In the days and weeks following the October 1987 Crash I heard many people say, 'Gee, Chase Corp at 200¢ – that's got to be cheap. All the lemmings are selling – I'll buy some more!' And they did buy more. Even while the sharemarket was falling there were people buying what they thought were very cheap assets – they were trying to pick the bottom. However, they only thought that they were cheap because of what they had been before. If Chase Corp had been $4 and now they were $2, that had to be cheap, didn't it? And if others were selling they should be buying – shouldn't they? Obviously not!

There was no analysis and little consideration – it was only a before-and-after comparison. (It is probably fair to say that few people in the market at that time had either the skills to do the analysis or the expertise to make the judgement.) In fact, things are far too confusing to do nothing but stand against the tide and do the opposite of what everyone else is doing – it is difficult at times to know which way the tide is running! As previously noted, in bear markets there are more up days than there are down days – it's just that the down days are bigger. Therefore in some bear markets you might find that standing against the crowd is actually selling, the very opposite of what you are intending.

> **It is difficult at times to know which way the tide is running!**

How then do you buy in gloom? How do you know to sell in boom?

The answer is to be a value investor.

VALUE INVESTING

This takes us right back to **Secret 3 – Buy for Yield**. As an investor you are buying earnings – as cheaply as possible. That needs to be kept firmly in view. You need to ignore the peripheral vision, ignore the many sideshows and focus clearly on your plan and what you are doing.

When some investors talk about a share or a property being cheap, they are not meaning that in absolute or dollar terms. They are in fact talking about it being cheap in terms of earnings – it is on a low P:E or high yield. A share trading at 70¢ may or may not be cheaper than one trading at 450¢ – you can't tell until you've looked at the earnings per share. In spite of that there are times when the inexperienced are attracted to 'cheap' shares, because they can buy lots of them. These people may know the price of their shares but not the value of them. In investment terms 'cheap' or 'expensive' are about earnings and value, not price.

If you have studied and analysed correctly, gloom presents what you want cheaper. If a property was a good buy at a 9% yield, it is a far better buy at an 11% yield. Provided nothing fundamental has changed relating to the property, to the lease, to the tenant or to market rentals, you should ignore the herds of gloom merchants and buy it.

> A value investor knows how much she should pay for those earnings, given their quality and sustainability.

This is backing yourself to be right. It might not be something for the new or inexperienced investor but it is a substantial part of why some people succeed. It is also the reason why others should, initially at least, play the averages – these are people who lack the skill, experience and judgement to successfully back themselves.

Investors are buying a stream of earnings – they want that stream to be a great as possible for the amount of money they are going to pay for it. Like any good trader, a value investor knows how much she should pay for those earnings, given their quality and sustainability and given what other earnings she could buy for the same money.

▼SPECIAL NOTE: TECHNICAL ANALYSIS

There are people who try to time markets by using 'technical analysis'. They are sometimes called 'chartists' because they produce charts and graphs to find patterns which will predict the future direction of the market. Technical analysts draw all sorts of different graphs and charts, tracing not just prices in the market but also volumes.

They have their own jargon – they look for 'double tops', 'heads and shoulders', 'resistance and support levels', 'break outs', etc – which gives them the same appearance as fringe religions and cults. Many fundamental investors are very sceptical regarding the performance and effectiveness of technical analysis – one of the oldest lines is that it has about the same efficiency as Roman augurs had in the study of oxen entrails (but, I suppose, a bit cleaner). That probably isn't quite fair. Certainly it is no substitute for fundamental analysis and the search for earnings. However, the study of patterns and trends while looking for signs that those trends might be broken or reversed has got to be of some interest.

Anyone who follows this to the exclusion of investment fundamentals is clearly a crank. Nevertheless, although I would never waste my time producing graphs or charts, I always find them quite interesting when one is put under my nose.

Investing (and timing) by value means thinking about the market that you are investing in, be it the bond, property or sharemarket. The first thing to answer is whether or not this particular market is undervalued or overvalued (or perhaps about right). To get an idea of how well your chosen market is valued, look at two things:

1. **Compare the average income which can come off the market with what can come off other markets.** For example, it may be that good quality commercial property yields are 8%, bonds are 6% and P:Es for quality share are 12 (giving an earnings rate of 8.5%). Assuming a reasonable economy for shares and property to perform in I would say that those two make better investments than bonds. However, if property yields fell to, say, 6.5% there would need to be a fairly good reason or your money should come out of that and into shares.

   This happens all the time in the markets and there always seems a good explanation for why an investment type deserves to sell at a high P:E or an especially low yield. These explanations can certainly be justified in the case of particular shares or properties – but seldom does an investment class move much outside its usual trading range and stay there. For example, in 1990 in New Zealand you could buy first class industrial properties at a yield of 14% – well above the normal range. Clearly that was a great time to buy and some people made themselves very rich as property prices rose to reflect more reasonable yields of around 9-10%.

2. **Compare your market to what earnings levels have applied historically.** This means looking at average yields and P:E ratios and comparing them to what have applied in the past. For example, in New Zealand, P:E ratios for good companies have usually been around 14–16 with only the very best warranting a price of 18–20 times earnings. However, through 1986–1987 P:Es of many companies were well into the 20s and 30s. Sir Robert Muldoon was right! Similarly, at the same time commercial property yields were as low as 5% against a historic norm of around 8%.

> **Seldom does an investment move much outside its usual trading range and stay there.**

Looking at and comparing these is partly a matter of experience and judgement but it has also been done statistically. Australian Austin Donnelly, in his book *Sensible Share Investing,* uses a database from his 35 years in the Australian sharemarket and puts dividend yields into 5 different zones ranging from 2.2% to a zone 5.5% and above. Donnelly shows that timing is both possible and practical. By buying when dividend yields are at historic highs the chances of good gains are very strong while the risk of downside is low. Donnelly backs up his own statistical work with a similar study done in the USA.

Such a method of picking investments to buy because their income is higher than usual is no surefire means of timing success which will ring a bell at the bottom of the market and another at the top of the market – no such system can ever exist. However, what it will do is provide a filter to screen out the worst excesses of the market. It will allow you to see good times to buy, if not the very best times; give you timing for the medium term, if not the short term.

SELLING

Timing the sale of your investments is the same as purchasing – only in reverse. It is no easier to sell in times of boom than it is to buy in times of gloom. The markets are just as noisy, the broker and expert comments just as forthright and the emotion of greed is just as strong as the emotion of fear.

The time to sell is when P:E ratios are high or property yields very low. This is not easy because the reason for these being unusually high or low is that the market is expecting income to rise strongly, thus justifying low initial earnings rates or yields. The market is anticipating such great growth that it is worthwhile to put up with a low return because of the huge profits or rents to be reaped in the future.

> **It is no easier to sell in times of boom than it is to buy in times of gloom.**

Experience shows that in spite of the hugely optimistic noises of many in the market, such profits or rents never quite arrive in the desired or required amount. I believe that it is quite justified to build into the price of investment markets some degree of anticipated income, but not blue sky. Note that this is a rule which applies more to markets overall than to individual investments. Particular properties or shares may be worth holding or buying: a property at a 5% yield if you are confident the rent will double fairly soon or a share at a P:E of 30 if you know that the profits are likely to increase by 25% a year for the next few years.

Although your best strategy is to hold investments long term, you should always be happy to sell them if they or the market become fundamentally unsound. Do not sell investments simply because they have risen in price – the chances are they will keep rising. Sell them if they have risen to a level that they are now unfairly priced (ie, expensive). Ask yourself if you would buy this investment at this price. If the answer is an emphatic 'no' then you should sell.

The other time to sell is when you have made a mistake. When this happens (and it will) don't spend time wishing and hoping, resolving to sell when (or if) the price goes back to a certain level. Instead forget your cost price and cut your losses. Get your money out of the mistake and into something which will work for you.

Investments are just pieces of paper or bricks and iron.

Successful investors always need to be in a frame of mind which allows them to sell on the basis of value (or lack of it). There is no room for loyalty or sentiment. Some people do get quite attached to their investments, especially those which have done well for them. Psychologists of the behaviourist school would say that the behaviour of investing has been rewarded and is therefore hard to reverse the behaviour and sell. However, that is what sometimes needs to be done, regardless of how you might feel about them (remember: feeling is not important – it's what you think about them that counts). Investments are just pieces of paper or bricks and iron, not deserving of any emotion or affection. They are there to serve you – when they no longer do, sell them.

APPENDIX 1

INVESTMENT DIRECTORY

BANK BILLS

These are a discounted 'Bill of Exchange'. This means two things:

▼ **The fact that it is a 'Bill of Exchange' makes it negotiable.**
The Bill is like a post dated cheque and can be traded before payment date. Like a postdated cheque the Bill is an order requiring payment from one party to another.

▼ **That the Bill is discounted reflects the interest to be paid.** If the drawer needs to borrow $150,000, he will issue a Bill for, say $151,025 to be presented for payment in 30 days' time. The borrower will receive the $150,000 which he is borrowing and hand over the postdated cheque (the Bill) for $151,025. The additional $1025 reflects the interest due to the lender.

This Bill for $151,025 may be traded on the money market. The party who has lent the money may be able to sell it for more or less than the $150,000 he paid for it, depending on which way interest rates go.

There are three main sorts of Bills:

▼ **Commercial Bills** – these are Bills between one corporate and another.

▼ **Bank Bills** – these are Bills that are 'accepted' by a bank, meaning that the bank will accept and pay out on the Bill on due date.

▼ **Treasury Bills** – the New Zealand Government will at times issue Bills to cover short-term financing.

Bills are usually issued for 30, 60, 90 or 180 days. While most people investing in Bills are large corporates, there are some private investors who make use of Bank bills. Provided that they are 'bank accepted', they are as safe as putting money in the bank and usually pay a little more interest than other bank deposits. Most people investing in Bills roll over their investment each expiry, getting a new interest rate depending upon the level at which the Bill market is trading at. Bills start at $50,000 but are probably more suitable for investors with over $250,000.

CASH MANAGEMENT TRUSTS

These are funds which invest in liquid assets (cash, Bills, certificates of deposit) to provide income for investors. Most try to obtain a better cash return than the investor would receive on-call at the bank. This is achieved by the fund manager operating in the wholesale money markets, using economies of scale to increase returns. A cash management trust allows investors to participate in markets which would otherwise be outside their scope.

Cash management trusts usually have most of their money in short-term securities. The bulk of the funds will be in Bills which mature within 90 days, with only some out to 12 months and perhaps a little in mortgages in order to increase return. Cash management trusts see considerable inflow and outflow of funds as investors use the trust for their short-term money. The trust needs to keep liquid so that it can redeem units at any time.

The fees for cash management trusts are usually low – there is relatively little work for the manager (compared to equities and property) and to give a return which will compete with bank deposits they need to be kept at this level. There is often little or no entry/exit fee and the ongoing management fees are usually comparatively small.

Cash management trusts are income trusts. All income is paid out to investors and there is no capital growth. They can be a good alternative to on-call bank deposits for many people and should be treated as such.

DEBENTURE STOCK

Debenture stock is an interest-earning deposit. An investor makes her investment and is given a debenture as security. A debenture secures the assets of a company (in the same way as a mortgage secures a property), ensuring that the debenture holders are paid in priority to other creditors.

The debenture is granted to a trustee who holds the debenture security on behalf of all of the stock-holding investors. The trustee acts as watchdog for the investors, overseeing the company on their behalf.

Most debenture stock is with finance companies. The deposit is usually a fixed-interest investment for anything from 3 months to 5 years.

The advantage of these types of investments is that they usually pay a higher interest rate than banks or other interest-earning deposits. The disadvantage is that in spite of the debenture security, there is greater risk. The debenture secures the assets of the finance company but other than the loans that the company has made, these assets are likely to be small (a bit of office furniture and some computers). In the event of failure, therefore, the investor will be dependent on the quality and standing of the finance company's loan book. If the investor does not have a first-ranking debenture, someone else (the first debenture holder, likely to be the finance company's bank or some other investor) is going to get their money back first which may leave a shortfall for the second- or third-ranking debenture stock. Having said that, finance companies do not fail very often. They usually work on very good profit margins, are aggressive in the marketplace and tend to make good profits. Nevertheless it would be unwise to have a large proportion of your funds in just one debenture stock, particularly if the debenture was lower ranking.

ENDOWMENT WARRANTS

Popular in Australia, these are starting to find favour amongst New Zealand investors who are looking for a geared equity investment.

Endowment warrants are usually long-term investments – 10 years is typical. The investor buys shares, putting up 50% of the price as a deposit and borrowing the balance. The idea is that the dividends from the shares pay off the loan, both the principle and interest. (Whether this happens of course depends on the performance of the shares.) All going well, at the end of 10 years the investor will have paid off the loan and will now own a block of shares without any borrowing.

In the event that the dividends do not pay off the loan, the investor must pay the balance outstanding or forfeit the shares.

EQUITY TRUSTS

Most equity trusts are open-ended unit trusts, although there are some closed trusts which are listed on the sharemarket. Equity trusts divide into two groups:

▼ **Passive funds** (see page 30).
▼ **Actively managed funds.**

Actively managed equity unit trusts work in the same way as other unit trusts. Investors pay into the fund and the manager invests the funds in equities as profitably as possible. Some equity fund managers have large research departments and spend a great deal of time going out to companies and assessing their worth as investments. This is of course expensive, making the management fees higher. However, in my view it is very necessary – if you are going to manage actively (rather than passively) you should do it properly. In assessing the fees that active funds charge, you should look at the value you are receiving, not just the price you are paying.

Equity trusts are based on just about every type of share investment imaginable: there are small company trusts, leaders' trusts, infrastructure trusts, growth trusts and a whole range of international equity trusts – emerging markets, Asia trusts, European funds, US trusts, etc. There are so many of these that you can end up with just about as many trusts as you would normally have shares (which rather defeats the purpose of trusts in simplifying and managing things for you). If you are going to hold equities through managed unit trusts you should try to do it through just one or two top-performing New Zealand equity funds and a couple of international ones.

Managed equity trusts are especially good for those who want to buy into international shares but have difficulty finding enough information and keeping up to date.

FORESTRY INVESTMENT

The business of growing trees can be very profitable. It is (almost) literally an investment where you plant an acorn and watch a mighty oak grow! Even without advantageous tax treatment, forestry investment would be popular – it is an investment which grows in size and value with each season. Forestry is seen by many as a 'real' investment – something which can be touched – and a part of New Zealand's valuable primary industry exports.

The first difficulty of forestry investment relates to the practical considerations of silviculture such as choosing land in areas which will show good growth, protecting the trees from disease and fire, correct pruning and thinning, and other forest management issues. These are such that most people quite rightly invest in forestry through a professionally managed syndicate.

The second difficulty is that it takes a long time for most useful trees to grow to maturity. The 25-30 years required is not a time-frame that everyone wants to invest for.

The third difficulty associated with the second one, is assessing the probable demand for forestry products in 25-30 years' time. The world is likely to be very different from what it is now in the year 2025 – who knows what material we might be using to build houses, make paper, etc?

The fourth difficulty is that forestry is largely an export industry. This brings in problems such as exchange rates, the economies of our customer countries and transport (wood products are bulky and heavy and New Zealand is a long way from everywhere).

Many of these difficulties are offset by this country's competitive advantages in growing trees. We have a good climate, good soil and an industry with many researchers and experts on silviculture. These mean that even a stable (let alone improving) demand/supply equation is likely to give very good long-term returns to investors.

However, the keys to forestry investment are the way it fits in well with most people's life cycle, and the tax treatment of such an investment.

Most people investing in forestry do so in their middle age. Someone at age 40 may well have a good job and salary, other income-earning investments, a tax problem and no need for any further immediate income. Such a person may want to invest for her later years, a time when she will have little other income. Forestry investment is ideal for this person.

There are three stages involved:

Forestry Investment time line

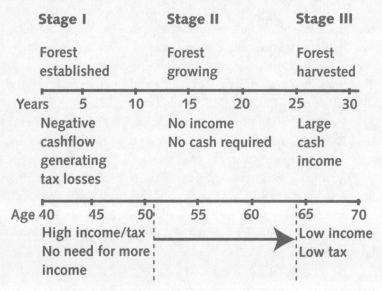

First of all, much of her investment input will be a tax-deductible expense because the funds are used for preparing, planting and establishing the forest. The only major expense which is not tax-deductible to forestry investors is the cost of the land. This is why many forestry investors effectively lease the forest land.

The other reason why this is a good idea is that it allows you to put more capital into trees, rather than land. In investing in forests you do not particularly want your money to go into property – not in any case property which might be remote and have little other use. A forest investment where the land is leased is often much more efficient – it is an investment where all of your funds have gone into trees and it is better for tax purposes.

Care is needed to ensure that ownership of your forest is structured correctly so that the tax losses can be accessed and offset against other income. Most professional forestry syndications are properly structured to achieve this. Proper structuring will mean that the investor will receive a tax refund cheque from the Inland Revenue Department.

The second stage is for a period of two or three decades, say from age 40 to age 65 or 70. During this period the forest grows but gives negligible or no income. That suits the investor because it is a period in her life where she has high income from her job or business and perhaps from other investments. It is a time when she wants capital growth, not income.

The third stage is when the forest matures. When it is harvested and the timber sold, the profits become taxable. By this time our investor may well have less income as she is working less or not at all – she may no longer be on the top marginal tax rate. The profits from forestry are assessable in the year that they are received – it may in some circumstances be possible to manipulate the timing so that the forest is sold in a low-income year, although this will not be possible if there is a syndicate and therefore a whole group of people to consider. The only thing which could be done would be to sell the share to another related party (family trust or spouse) in a low- or no-income year, thus crystallising at least part of the profit in that advantageous year.

Forestry investment suits many people because of tax and life-cycle issues. However, growing trees is not a business without risk – forests can fail, there are industry risks and the markets for its products are volatile. It is not an area therefore to which you should be overexposed.

LIFE BONDS

Life bonds are a managed investment which also has life assurance attached to it. The money that you pay in is not only an investment but covers a life assurance premium. Often the life assurance is only a very small part of the investment.

This investment took advantage of life insurance companies' tax regime which meant that once the companies had paid tax on all profits at 33%, their policyholders received their bonuses tax paid. This was most advantageous for superannuitants who were subject to surcharge. Much of the popularity of life bonds (hundreds of millions of dollars have gone into them over the last few years) has been to minimise this surcharge.

In spite of the large amounts of money that have gone into life bonds and the correspondingly large amount of surcharge avoided, the Government never moved to close off this loophole. Many life bonds have such a small component of life assurance that they were clearly an anti-surcharge device. Presumably the unpopularity of the surcharge made it impossible politically for the Government to act against life bonds.

Now that the surcharge has been abolished, the popularity of life bonds is likely to decline rapidly.

LISTED INVESTMENT TRUSTS

These are closed trusts that are listed on the stock exchange. They are closed in the sense that once a set number of units has been issued, they are closed to any more investors buying in – the number of units on issue is finite and disclosed.

The units in LITs are not redeemable by the manager of the trust. Once you have purchased units, the only way that you can cash up is to sell them on the sharemarket. The manager never values the units with a view to buying the units back from investors, as happens with unlisted unit trusts. Instead the units are simply bought and sold by investors like shares. Obviously the price of units on the stock exchange will tend to reflect the underlying value of the trust's assets but it will not necessarily reflect that exactly –

the unit's price may vary and fluctuate as investors take a view on the future performance of the trust's assets.

LITs in New Zealand are either property trusts or equity trusts. The best known ones are probably Foreign and Colonial Investments and Templeton Emerging Markets (these are equity trusts) and Kiwi Income Property Trust and AMP Office Trust (for property).

The manager of an LIT is not involved when an investor buys into a trust and therefore makes no entry or exit charge. However, as an investor you will have the costs of your sharebroker in both purchasing and selling – these could be similar to the costs charged by an open unit trust. The ongoing management fees for an LIT may be a little cheaper than an unlisted trust as there is less administration.

The main advantage of an LIT is that it is not vulnerable to a run on funds as closed unit trusts can be. At times in both New Zealand and Australia large numbers of investors have tried to redeem their units from an open unit trust manager only to overwhelm the trust's liquidity and force it to sell assets. An LIT has no such problem – investors buy and sell in an open-market transaction and that is of no concern to the trust itself. An LIT does not have to hold significant cash reserves to redeem investors' units and therefore can be fully invested in the investment area of its choice, whether equities or property. The disadvantage of an LIT is that because it is listed on the sharemarket it is subject in the short term to the vagaries and volatility of that market, and will show more volatility.

MASTER TRUSTS

The idea of a Master Trust is to simplify the paperwork for those who want to invest in several different investment areas through several different unit trusts. Although unit trusts save you the administration of investing directly yourself, anyone who is invested in, say, 10 unit trusts will still have quite a lot of work keeping track of the paperwork.

The Master Trust solves this by centralising everything. You invest only in the Master Trust which in turn invests in the desired individual trusts. This means that you write just one cheque (to the Master Trust) and receive only one set of reports (from the Master Trust). In addition you will be able to swap your investments in the underlying trusts at low or no cost through the Master Trust.

Of course, the addition of the Master Trust adds a whole new layer of management:

However, the cost of this new management layer is offset by the Master Trust dealing in large amounts of money and therefore being able to negotiate lower management fees with the managers of the individual trusts. These rates are usually lower than what an individual investor could get, making the overall cost about the same as if you invested in a range of trusts yourself. In effect, you are getting the centralised record-keeping from the Master Trust for nothing.

The first promoter of a Master Trust in New Zealand was Money Managers with their First Masterfund. Within two years it had attracted many millions of dollars and some competition showing that there are many investors who would prefer someone else to have their administrative hassle.

MORTGAGE INCOME TRUST

This is a trust which invests in mortgages, trying to give investors a better income than they would get on term deposit at the bank. Some mortgage income trusts are quite large, having hundreds of millions of dollars invested and with a spread of lending across many types of property – residential, commercial and farming. Their lending criteria are usually fairly conservative, keeping their bad debt levels low.

Mortgage income trusts usually pay out all their income to investors – there is no capital growth. The fees are relatively low, helping them to compete satisfactorily with bank deposits.

The main difficulty that some mortgage income trusts have is to stay fully invested in mortgages. Marketing to encourage people to take out a mortgage and borrow is difficult and expensive. Mortgage income trusts want as much of their funds in higher yield mortgages as possible rather than on call at the bank while they wait for someone to take it off their hands. When the trust's percentage of bank deposits rises (and the percentage of the funds mortgages falls) the returns to investors drop accordingly.

PROPERTY TRUSTS

Most fund managers offer an investment vehicle based on commercial and industrial property. In New Zealand these are largely open-ended unit trusts, although there are some where the structure is that of a closed investment trust which is listed on the stock exchange (see *Listed Investment Trusts*). This structure is very common in Australia.

Most property unit trusts have high fees – both the entry fees and the ongoing management fees are usually greater than most other unit trusts. These high charges reflect the very real and substantial costs of purchasing and managing investment property. Direct property investors should take note – property is expensive to manage, either in terms of money or in time. Many direct property investors do not recognise how expensive property management is because they do so much themselves. Only when someone is paid to do all the purchasing, managing, accounting and selling does the full cost of property investment become apparent.

Most property trusts are fairly lowly geared (they have little in the way of borrowings). This means that they provide investors with both income and capital growth. However, the low gearing means that the capital growth might be less than what you would expect.

Property trusts are sometimes quite large and this gives two main advantages:

▼ They can go into the quality end of the market, which is often too expensive for private investors.

▼ They can have a range of properties (industrial, retail and commercial) and are not exposed to just one major tenant.

The major disadvantage of a property trust is that it is not as tax efficient as direct property investment. Private property investors are able to claim many costs (eg, home/office, travel, subscriptions, telephone, etc) because they are in the business of renting property. This is not available to unit trust investors. In addition, there are some New Zealand property investors who, being more aggressive, prefer their property portfolio to be more highly geared, thus giving less taxable income but more tax-free capital growth.

UNIT TRUSTS

A unit trust is probably the most common form of managed fund in New Zealand. Like all managed funds, it works by pooling investors' funds which are then managed and invested for them. Unit trusts are 'open-ended' which means they can continue to issue more units to investors according to demand. Unlike closed trusts which are listed on the stock exchange (see *Listed Investment Trusts*) open-ended trusts have no limit on the number of units issued.

There are three parties involved:

1. **Investors** – people who pay into the trust either in one lump sum or (as many trusts allow) monthly.

2. **The Trustees** – one of the six Permanent Trust Companies (their operations are governed by statute) hold the funds in trust. They act as a watchdog, making sure that funds are invested in accordance with the trust deed.

3. **The Manager** – someone (often a bank or life company) who
    supposedly has great investment skill and expertise invests
    the trust's funds. The manager has usually promoted the
    trust (or trusts – most managers have a range of them) from
    the beginning and carries on promoting and advertising to
    bring in new investors.

Both the trustee and the manager get paid for their services –
the manager more than the trustee, which reflects the respective
amounts of work required.

When the trust is formed, it is 'unitised' – that is, the trust is
divided into units which can be bought by investors. The trust can
continue to issue new units, theoretically at least forever. The value
of the units rises and falls as the value of the trust's assets
appreciates or depreciates. New investors buy into the trust at the
manager's valuation, which is made at regular intervals. These
values are often published in newspapers and magazines. There is
often both an entry price and an exit price for unit trusts, one the
price at which you can purchase units, the other the price at which
you can cash up your units. The difference between the two, which
might range from 1% to 5%, represents an upfront sales fee which
the manager receives but usually passes on to the broker who sold
the units. With negotiation you can get that sales fee waived or at
least reduced.

Unit trusts may be based on property, equities, mortgages,
bonds, etc, or they may be a diversified balanced fund. *Growth trusts*
are predominantly invested in shares and property – they may
pay out a little income to investors from rents and dividends but
most of the return to the investor is in the growth in the value
of the units as the underlying assets appreciate. *Income trusts*
invest in deposits, bills, bonds and mortgages and pay out all of
their income.

The trust is governed by a Trust Deed, a document of many
pages which spells out the objectives of the trust, what it is to invest
in and how it is to be managed. The trustee oversees the manager,
ensuring that he acts appropriately and in accordance with the
deed.

Unit trusts are good for investors who do not want to invest their own funds. They allow you to invest in one particular area or to have a diversified investment.

A variation on unit trusts which are offered by trust companies are *group investment* funds (see page 203).

WARRANTS

Warrants are a leveraged sharemarket investment. The purchase of a warrant gives the holder the right to buy a share at a certain price (the *strike price*) on or before a certain date. The holder of the warrant does not have the obligation to purchase the share – at exercise date, the holder can simply throw the warrant in the rubbish bin if the price of the underlying share has not reached the strike price. Obviously he will have lost the money that he paid for the warrant but does not have to compound that loss by buying a share for more than he could buy it on the sharemarket.

Warrants are usually issued by merchant banks. They usually purchase a block of shares (often several hundred thousand, or even millions) and put them away (presumably in their vaults). They then sell off warrants to investors, the price that they receive covering their financing costs for holding the shares and their profit margin (the bank also gets dividends over that time). The warrants are then listed on the sharemarket so that the investors can sell their warrants if they want before maturity date. When the exercise date arrives the investor can either exercise the warrant (in which case the merchant bank receives the payment and hands over the share scrip) or write off their capital outlay on the warrant (in which case the merchant bank is stuck with the shares).

Clearly the bank is carrying a risk in holding the shares – there is a race against time for the shares to reach the strike price or beyond. However, that is a risk that the merchant bank has been paid to take and it is alleviated by issuing only warrants for top quality, leading shares.

From the investor's point of view, he gets a sharemarket investment which is geared and with the downside limited to what he has paid for the warrant. He does not have to go anywhere near a bank manager nor pay interest (although he receives no dividends, either). All of his profit is a capital one and will usually be tax free.

The best known warrants in New Zealand are issued by Deutsche Bank, although SBC Warburg also offers some. They are only issued on leading companies, some of which are New Zealand, some Australian. A typical warrant is over Colonial Ltd. The warrant expires on 25 February 1999 and has an exercise price of A$4.00. At the time of writing Colonial Ltd shares were trading at A$4.40 and the warrant was trading at $0.42¢.

APPENDIX 2

GLOSSARY OF INVESTMENT TERMS

Abnormal items – a transaction that does not usually happen in a company but which in any particular period has been unusually large.

Accruals rules – accounting rules which adjust a company's accounts so that items are accounted for when income or expenditure is incurred or committed, rather than when cash changes hands.

Aggressive – prepared to tolerate greater investment risk.

Amortisation – when a company systematically reduces the value of an asset in its books.

Appreciation – the rise in the value of an asset.

Arbitrage – taking advantage of a difference between the market for an asset and the derivative market of the same asset or a difference between two markets (eg, Australian Stock Exchange and New Zealand Stock Exchange). This entails buying in one while simultaneously selling in the other to make a profit.

Asset – anything which can be owned and which has a financial value.

Asset stripping – buying a company below its asset value and then selling off the assets to make a profit.

At call deposit – a deposit which must be repaid immediately on demand.

Audit – the independent checking and verifying of a company's accounts. All companies listed on the stock exchange must have their accounts audited.

Bank bill – a tradeable security, issued by a bank on behalf of a company for a set amount of money. Usually these are 'bank accepted' or 'endorsed', meaning a bank is effectively guaranteeing payment. Bank bills are for 30, 60, 90 or 180 days, and the smallest amount is $100,000. Banks trade these bills on the wholesale money markets in parcels of $1 million.

Basis point – one hundredth of one percent.

Bear – a pessimist who believes a market will fall and who is a seller. Bears claw markets down.

Beta – a measure of an asset's historical movement or volatility compared with a related index. For example, if a share moved 12% when the index moved 10% it would have a Beta factor of 1.2 (a ratio of 12:10).

Bid – an offer to buy at a price.

Blue chip – a share which is regarded as the best quality. Usually those of large older companies, they do not always perform the best even though they are regarded as solid and reliable.

Bond – a fixed-interest investment usually issued by governments, local authorities or larger corporates for periods of up to 10 years in New Zealand. Are usually able to be traded on a secondary market, allowing the investor to cash up before maturity date if desired.

Bonus issue – when shares are issued free to existing shareholders. Shareholders are not necessarily any better off because the extra shares dilute the assets and earnings per share accordingly.

Bourse – French for *stock exchange*. The original 'bourse' was in

Belgium and closed in 1998 after 500 years of trading.

Brokerage – the fee charged by a sharebroker for buying or selling securities (shares, bonds, etc). Usually 1-1.5% of the amount transacted.

Bull – an optimist who believes that the market will rise and who is a buyer. Bulls toss the market up with their horns.

Call option – the holder has the right to buy a share at a given strike price up until a certain date.

Capital – the original, basic funds used to invest. Capital is like a tree, income is its fruit.

Capital asset pricing model – a theory which prices investments by adding a premium according to risk. Shows the relationship between expected return and risk.

Capitalisation rate – used by property investors to value investment properties by their yield. Used synonymously with *yield*.

Cash box – a company that has no assets other than a lot of cash.

Certificate of deposit – a promise by a bank to pay a particular amount on a due date.

Chartists – those who try to predict the future direction of a market by studying graphs and charts. Charting is called *technical analysis*.

Commercial bill – a bill of exchange that has not been endorsed (guaranteed) by a bank. These carry greater risks and therefore yield a better return to investors.

Compound interest – the adding of interest paid to the original capital to get even more interest.

Contract note – a note sent by your broker confirming what has been bought or sold on your behalf.

Convertible note – a security issued by a company giving a fixed-interest rate but which can be converted to shares.

Correction – when a market reverses its previous trend. A correction is usually thought of as a short-term break before the original trend resumes. Just when a 'correction' becomes serious and is called a 'crash' is a matter of debate at the time.

Coupon rate – the rate of interest that a bond originally paid when it was first sold. Years ago bonds had coupons that the investor tore off on the stated date and received cash as interest. If the bond has traded on the secondary market to another investor, the coupon (or original) rate is likely to be different from the new effective rate.

Credit rating – the measurement of a person's or an organisation's creditworthiness and likely ability to fulfil financial obligations.

Creditor – someone who is owed money. If you have some money in the bank, you are a creditor of the bank. If you owe the bank, the bank is your creditor.

Cum dividend – with dividend. Shares being traded cum dividend come with the right to receive an upcoming dividend payment.

Debenture – a type of security given by a company to someone who is lending it money. Often also used to mean *debenture stock* – an investment (usually fixed interest) which is secured by way of a debenture.

Debtor – someone who owes money. If you have money in the bank, the bank is your debtor.

Depreciate – to fall in value.

Depreciation – a non-cash expense which companies can charge in their accounts. Companies (and others) can depreciate their assets by a set amount each year for tax purposes. This does not affect the company's cashflow but reduces profit and therefore tax.

Derivatives – 'virtual' investments whose value 'derives' from the value of some other, 'real' investments. See *Futures*.

Discounted value – the value that an investor pays for a bank bill, commercial bill or certificate of deposit. This is less than he will receive on due date, that difference reflecting his interest rate.

Distraint – a clause in commercial and industrial leases which allows the landlord to seize the tenant's goods for unpaid rent. Not permissible for residential leases.

Dividend – the part of a company's profits which are paid out to shareholders in cash.

Dividend yield – the percentage return an investor will get from dividends. Care must be taken to see whether the yields are 'gross' (ie, before tax) or 'net' (after tax). Some publications use one but not the other.

Dividend imputation – a device to ensure that investors do not pay tax twice. The dividend which is paid will have *imputation credits* to the extent that the company has paid tax. If the company has paid the full rate of tax on all its profit the dividend will be 100% imputed and the investor will pay no more tax. If the company has not paid the full rate of tax the dividend will be partly imputed and the investor will need to pay what is effectively the balance.

Don't sell notice – a notice that companies are required to make to the stock exchange which might affect the value of the shares. It usually means that a takeover or some other major transaction is underway.

Dual listing – when a company is listed on two stock exchanges, such as New Zealand and Australia.

Earnings per share (eps) – the amount of profit which is attributable to each share in a company. Calculated by dividing the company's earnings (profit) by the number of shares on issue. If a company has 100 million shares on issue and makes a profit of $15 million its earnings per share is:

$$\frac{\$15 \text{ million}}{100 \text{ million}} = 15\cent \text{ per share}$$

Earnings yield – the amount of profit as a percentage of the share price that each share yields. Calculated by dividing the eps by the share price. For example, if a company had an eps of 15¢ per share and its share price was 140¢, its earnings yield would be:

$$\frac{15¢}{140¢} \times 100 = 10.71\%$$

Elliot wave theory – a form of charting (technical analysis) which says that markets rise in five major waves and then fall in three waves. The theory gained some notoriety in New Zealand through a sharemarket newsletter which based most of its recommendations (including one in 1987 to sell all New Zealand shares) on the Elliot wave theory.

Endowment policy – a life insurance policy which also has a savings component. The capital plus bonuses are paid out on the death of the holder or on a set date.

Equity – the part of an asset that you own, that is, your share. You hold equity in a company when you buy shares. It is also used in the sense that your equity in a property is the total value of the property less any borrowings.

Exposure – the risk and return that you have by owning something. When you buy shares you are 'exposed' to equities. You may also be exposed to certain risks by doing things – by not going on a fixed rate for your borrowings, you are 'exposed' to interest rate fluctuations.

Ex-dividend – a share which no longer has the right to a dividend payment is said to have gone 'ex-dividend'.

Extraordinaries – transactions which are outside a company's usual course of business.

Fee simple – freehold land with absolute ownership.

Face value – the amount of principal that will be paid on due date. Used especially in bonds, the face value may be different to what you pay on the secondary market.

Final dividend – companies often make two dividend payments, the interim dividend and the final dividend. Adding the two together gives the annual dividend payout and this figure is used to calculate the dividend yield.

Fixed interest – an investment which pays a set amount of interest until maturity.

Float – a company offering its shares for sale, usually listing on the sharemarket at the same time.

Fully paid shares – shares in a company on which no further payments are due. These contrast with *contributing shares* or *receipts* which are only partly paid and to which shareholders may need to pay additional amounts in the future to convert to fully paid shares.

Futures – a futures contract is an agreement to buy and sell a set amount of standardised commodity at some point in the future. These contracts are traded on the futures market.

Gearing – borrowing money to buy an income-earning asset.

Gilt-edged – an old term for a quality investment, especially a bond.

Going public – when a company offers its shares to the public, usually floating on the Stock Exchange.

Government stock – bonds issued by the Government to finance its operations. Usually issued for 5-10 years they pay a fixed rate of interest, are traded on the secondary market and are regarded as the safest of investments.

Gross – an amount before deductions, especially of tax.

Gross yield – the dividend (or other cash return) before tax.

Group investment funds – a managed fund like a unit trust which is offered by one of the permanent trustee companies. They differ from unit trusts in that they do not need a separate manager and trustee and some of their income is taxed differently.

Hedging – using *synthetics* or *derivatives* to offset any possible loss.

Interim dividend – the dividend that is paid by a company mid-year. It is usually smaller than the final dividend.

Inverse yield curve – also called *negative yield curve*, it describes a situation where short-term interest rates are higher than long-term ones.

Index – a measure of the way a market changes over time. Sharemarket indices are the value of a basket of defined shares – as the value of those shares change, so too does the index.

Junk bonds – bonds issued by corporates which do not have a very high credit rating.

LAQC – loss attributing qualifying company. A special type of company which allows any tax losses to be taken directly to the shareholders. Very useful for property investors.

Lessee – someone who takes on a lease – the tenant.

Lessor – someone who grants a lease – the landlord.

Leverage – see *Gearing*.

Liabilities – debts owed by companies (or individuals).

Life insurance bonds – a managed investment fund which qualifies as a life insurance policy. The investment fund is taxed at 33% and any withdrawal is capital growth and not part of an investor's income. These were very useful to older investors to minimise the superannuation surcharge.

Liquid assets – anything that can quickly be turned into cash (eg, bonds tradeable on the secondary market, certificates of deposit).

Long – being a buyer (or a holder) on the futures market.

Managed funds – unit trusts, group investment funds, syndicates, superannuation schemes, etc, where money from investors is pooled and managed by a professional.

Margin – deposit paid by an investor who is borrowing to buy shares or futures contracts.

Maturity – the date that an investment (especially a bond or a bill) falls due for payment.

Money markets – not just one place but a network of computer and telephone trading of bank bills, government stock, treasury bills, etc. Also called 'capital markets' because it is where capital is bought and sold. The traders are usually banks, corporates, insurance companies, finance companies, etc.

Mortgage – a form of security but also used to mean a loan.

Mortgagee – the lender, who takes a mortgage for security.

Mortgagor – the borrower, who grants a mortgage as security.

Mortgage-free – a property which has no mortgage on it. Sometimes the word 'freehold' is used incorrectly to mean the same.

Mutual fund – American term for *managed fund*.

Negative gearing – borrowing to an extent where the income from the investment does not cover the interest.

Negative yield curve – see *Inverse yield curve*.

Negotiable security – one which can be bought or sold.

Net – an amount after all deductions.

Net yield – the after-tax return on an investment.

Nominal value – see *Face value*.

Odd lot – a small parcel of shares (usually under 100 shares).

Off market – the sale of some shares not made on the stock exchange.

Offer – a quote to sell a share.

Opportunity cost – the loss brought about by doing something else.

Options – the right to buy (*Call option*) or the right to sell (*Put option*) a security at a certain price on or before a certain date. Although there is the right to buy or sell there is not any obligation to do so.

Ordinary shares – shares which have been fully paid and which have voting rights and rights to dividends and capital on winding up.

Overcapitalise – especially concerned with property investment, overcapitalising means putting too good a building on a site.

Over-rented – a property whose rent is above the fair market rent. Usually the rent has been set some years previously when times were buoyant and it is held up there by a ratchet clause in the lease.

Over-subscribe – when a company floats some shares and finds that there are more buyers than there are shares available. Great for stags.

Paper profits – profits brought about by the appreciation of an asset which have not yet been realised (made real) by selling. Many would say that there is no such thing as a 'paper profit'. There is no profit until the cash has been banked.

Penny dreadful – a share which trades for just a few cents. Highly speculative, they usually have little or no asset backing or income.

Perpetual bond – a bond which pays income forever – it has no maturity date.

PIF – Property Investors' Federation. Most centres have a branch of the PIF. Well worth joining.

Preference shares – shares which get preference before ordinary shares for dividend payments or return of capital in liquidation. Preference shares rank behind creditors of a company but before ordinary shareholders.

Primary market – the issuing of a bond or a bill by the original borrower to the first investor. This may in some cases be able to be sold on the secondary market to another investor. Some bonds will be sold many times before maturity.

Price:Earnings ratio – the number of times that annual earnings per share (tax-paid profits) go into the share price. For example, a company which has a share price of 140¢ and is making 15¢ per share has a P:E ratio of

$$\frac{\text{share price}}{\text{eps}} = \frac{140¢}{15¢} = 9.3$$

Profit taking – realising profits after having a good run. Usually results in a 'technical correction' – a short-term down trend.

Property development – the activity of constructing buildings or subdividing land into sections and selling them off for a profit.

Property trust – a managed fund based on investment in commercial or industrial property.

Pyramiding – using the increased equity from unrealised capital gains to borrow more money to buy more investments. Used widely by property investors who get new valuations as often as possible to gear up to buy more property, and by margin traders.

Quote – an offer or a bid – ie, an asking price to sell, or a buying offer.

Ratchet clause – a clause in most commercial and industrial leases which allows the rent to rise but not to fall. Very much in the landlord's favour.

Rent – payment by a tenant to an owner. There are two types:
    1. **Gross rent** – this includes all the landlord's direct costs (rates, insurance, maintenance). The landlord has to meet these out of the gross rent. Most common in residential property.
    2. **Net rent** – the rent which is net in the landlord's hands after all direct costs have been met. Many commercial and industrial leases require a net rent to be paid – ie, the tenant pays not only the rent but also many of the direct costs such as rates and insurance.

Real return – the return an investor gets after both tax and inflation.

Redeemable share – a redeemable share is one where the company will redeem the share in cash at the end of a given period.

Research house – specialist firm whose role is to research investments. Mostly they advise the advisers. The two largest in New Zealand are IPAC Securities and FPG Research.

Resident withholding tax – rather like PAYE for wage and salary earners. When an investor is paid interest, the lender is required to deduct tax from the payments. This amount is offset against the tax which is assessed at the end of the year.

Roll-over – the renewal of a loan on substantially the same terms.

Run – a large number of depositors losing confidence in a bank and all trying to withdraw their money at the same time. Not a lot of fun if you are a banker.

Sale and leaseback – an arrangement where a property owner sells a property and at the same time leases it back from the new owner. Happens mostly with industrial property.

Scrip – share certificates.

Secondary market – a market where securities that have already been issued are bought and sold.

Securities – documents promising and securing the repayment of money or giving ownership. Usually these are tradeable and cover such things as bonds, share certificates, treasury bills, bank bills, etc.

Securitisation – banks or insurance companies bundling together a number of mortgages to sell them to an investor in one package.

Share certificate – a document certifying ownership of a number of shares. Soon to become a thing of the past with 'scripless trading'.

Share register – a register of all of the shareholders of a company, usually kept by a specialist firm of registry managers. The register is a document open to the public.

Short – has two meanings:
1. Short term.
2. Selling 'short' of an asset – ie, selling the asset before you have bought it in the expectation or hope that it will fall in value.

Simple interest – the interest due on a debt for a period and which is not compounded.

Speculator – someone who cares only about price movements and not about income from assets.

Spread – the difference between buy and sell quotes.

Stag – someone who buys shares when a company is floated, intending to sell as soon as they list on the sharemarket.

Stamp duty – a government tax paid on all property sales other than residential property. It is levied at 1% to $100,000 of the property's price and 2% thereafter.

Standard deviation – a statistical measurement of volatility.

Stock – in New Zealand this usually means a bond (as in 'Government stock'). In most other parts of the world it means a share.

Surrender value – the amount that a life company will pay if you surrender your policy before it expires.

Synthetics – 'virtual' investments, whose value is determined by some future event. See *Futures*.

Technical analysis – see *Chartist*.

Technical correction – a correction which is thought (hoped!) not to last very long or be very severe.

Term deposit – a bank deposit for an agreed term at an agreed interest rate.

Thick market – a very busy market with lots of participants.

Thin market – a market with very few participants and not much activity. This sort of market can be dangerous as it takes very few people and only a little money to push it far one way or the other.

Treasury Bills – often called T-Bills. Short-term borrowings by the Government which can be traded on the secondary market.

Triple witching hour – a day each quarter when three major synthetic (futures) markets mature. Can cause big price movements as traders and speculators have to close out their positions by buying (if they are *short)* or selling (if they are *long*).

Trustee – one who owns assets for the benefit of others. Acts as a watchdog for investors, ensuring proper management of the fund.

Underlet – a property which is let at below market rental.

Unit trust – a managed fund which pools investments. Funds are held by a trustee which 'unitises' them so that investors hold units. The trust is managed by a specialist investment or fund manager.

Vacant possession – a property which is not occupied or leased.

White elephant – a building with little use and therefore little value.

Wholesale money markets – computer trading network for securities over $1 million. Institutional investors are the only participants.

Yield – the percentage cash return on an investment.

Yield curve – a graph which plots the yield for investments of the same risk over different maturity dates.

Zero coupon bonds – a discounted bond which pays no interest. These were very tax effective (until the law was changed) because no interest meant no tax. The investor got a return through the fact that she purchased the bond at a discount to its face value.

APPENDIX 3

BIBLIOGRAPHY

Below is a small selection of books, magazines and periodicals which investors may find useful. I have included only books that I think will be helpful, excluding many which are unnecessary or not worthwhile. Some of the books are from overseas (often from Australia) and need to be read with local differences in mind. Do not forget your local newspaper or publications like *National Business Review* and *The Independent* as sources of good information – they usually have up-to-date news articles and feature more general articles on investment issues.

GENERAL INVESTMENT READING
Books

Five Rituals of Wealth, Tod Barnhart (Harper Publishing, 1995)
An American book, not as good as the title suggests, but it has some useful if basic information.

Personal Investment, Brian Birchall (Canterbury University Press)
Published in 1993, this is a well-written primer for new investors.

The Language of Money, Edna Carew (Allen & Unwin, 1988)
A dictionary of financial terms from Australia, but with good application in New Zealand.

Understanding Unit Trusts, Charles Beelaerts and Kevin Forde (Wrightbooks, 1994)
Australian, but gives a thorough account of the workings of unit trusts.

Making the Most of Your Money, Murray Weatherston (Viking, 1991)

A very good general guide to money issues, including investment. Out of print but probably available at libraries.

Personal Financial Planning for New Zealanders, Ed Vos (Dunmore Press, 1996)

Quite expensive at $49.95 and really more of a textbook for financial planners and advisers. However, it does contain some of the detailed formulae for risk analysis and bond/share/option valuation which serious investors might want.

Periodicals

New Zealand Investors' Monthly, (Equity Research, PO Box 27-288, Auckland)

Available by subscription or in news-stands, this is a good general publication for those especially interested in managed funds or equities (Equity Research does advertise itself extensively throughout).

PROPERTY INVESTMENT

Books

Jones on Property, Bob (Sir Robert) Jones

Out of print (and out of date) but a great read to see the mind of New Zealand's best known property investor and the entrepreneurial spirit in practice. Borrow a copy if you can.

Understanding Investment Property, N. E. Renton (The Investment Library, 1992)

Australian book of interest to new investors and serious professional investors alike. The second edition (1992) is quite large (290 pages) and covers everything for direct investors and for those buying into property trusts.

Building Wealth Through Investment Property, Jan Somers and Dolf de Roos (de Roos Associates, 1997)

Originally written by Jan Somers for Australia and adapted for New Zealand by Dr de Roos, this book has been immensely popular. It is mostly for residential investors. There is a great deal on how much money can be made in property investment and how it works, but little about any risks or difficulties involved.

Property Investment in New Zealand – A Strategy for Wealth, Martin Hawes (Shoal Bay Press, 1996)

Periodicals

Estate Magazine, (NZ Property Investors' Federation)
    A quarterly magazine mostly for residential property investors, it is the voice of the New Zealand Property Investors' Association (PO Box 3931, Christchurch). It is free when you join the association and contains many articles of interest to property investors.

Residential Property Investor Magazine
    Again, mostly for residential investors. This is a publication which is well worth getting. It contains detailed statistics of both rentals and sales throughout New Zealand along with some very good up-to-date editorial content. If you are interested in investing in residential property you should subscribe.

SHAREMARKET INVESTMENT
Books

Sensible Share Investing, Austin Donnelly (Wrightbooks, 1996)
    Australian, but a must for all sharemarket investors. Donnelly has a database going back over 30 years and experience to match. He uses both to very good effect. Donnelly has written over 40 books in that time and this must be one of his best.

Bemused Investor's Guide to Company Accounts in New Zealand, Bill Jamieson (Shoal Bay Press, 1998)
    Another really good book for anyone interested in investing intelligently in shares. It uses real examples of New Zealand companies and explains accounting and accounts well.

Shorten the Odds, Nigel McCarter (The Dunmore Press, 1997)

A book for someone who insists on the do-it-yourself approach. This book uses McCarter's own experiences in the market, both good and bad. A good buy for the serious sharemarket investor who does not want to rely on advisers.

Understanding Investment – The New Zealand Sharemarket, Ron Bennetts and John Cobb (Hodder Moa Beckett, 1991)

A very slim volume, adequate for beginning sharemarket investors only.

The New Zealand Company Register, (Mercantile Gazette Marketing)

This is an annual publication and includes a listing on every company on the New Zealand Stock Exchange. Each company has a page including abbreviated financial information (going back 10 years), major shareholders, directors, management personnel, issued capital and a commentary on the company's business activities. All share investors need a resource like this.

Periodicals

New Zealand Sharemarket Letter, (PO Box 30-264, Lower Hutt)

A fortnightly newsletter which I think is the best of its kind. Not only does each issue have commentary and recommendations but it carries the ratios, dividend yields, etc, for every company on the stock exchange. It also lists the profit results for each company as they are announced, making it a great historic record.

Shares, (469 La Trobe Street, Melbourne, Australia)

Australian, but very good!

INDEX